W9-ABG-223

PRECISION JOURNALISM

The SAGE CommText Series

Series Editor:
EVERETTE E. DENNIS
Gannett Center for Media Studies, Columbia University

Founding Editor: F. GERALD KLINE, *late of the School of Journalism and Mass Communication, University of Minnesota*
Founding Associate Editor: SUSAN H. EVANS, *Annenberg School of Communications, University of Southern California*

The **SAGE CommText** series brings the substance of mass communication scholarship to student audiences by blending syntheses of current research with applied ideas in concise, moderately priced volumes. Designed for use both as supplementary readings and as "modules" with which the teacher can "create" a new text, the **SAGE CommTexts** give students a conceptual map of the field of communication and media research. Some books examine topical areas and issues; others discuss the implications of particular media; still others treat methods and tools used by communication scholars. Written by leading researchers with the student in mind, the **SAGE CommTexts** provide teachers in communication and journalism with solid supplementary materials.

Available in this series:

1. TELEVISION IN AMERICA
   George Comstock
2. COMMUNICATION HISTORY
   John D. Stevens and Hazel Dicken Garcia
3. PRIME-TIME TELEVISION:
   Content and Control
   Muriel G. Cantor
4. MOVIES AS MASS COMMUNICATION
   Garth Jowett and James M. Linton
5. CONTENT ANALYSIS: An Introduction to Its Methodology
   Klaus Krippendorff
6. INTERPERSONAL COMMUNICATION:
   The Social Exchange Approach
   Michael E. Roloff
7. THE CARTOON: Communication to to the Quick
   Randall P. Harrison
8. ADVERTISING AND SOCIAL CHANGE
   Ronald Berman
9. COMPARATIVE COMMUNICATION RESEARCH
   Alex S. Edelstein
10. MEDIA ANALYSIS TECHNIQUES
    Arthur Asa Berger
11. SHAPING THE FIRST AMENDMENT:
    The Development of Free Expression
    John D. Stevens
12. THE SOAP OPERA
    Muriel G. Cantor and Suzanne Pingree
13. THE DISSIDENT PRESS: Alternative Journalism in American History
    Lauren Kessler
14. TELEVISION AND CHILDREN: A Special Medium for a Special Audience
    Aimée Dorr
15. PRECISION JOURNALISM:
    A Practical Guide
    David Pearce Demers and Suzanne Nichols
16. PUBLIC RELATIONS:
    What Research Tells Us
    John V. Pavlik
17. NEW ELECTRONIC PATHWAYS:
    Videotex, Teletext, and Online Databases
    Jerome Aumente
18. THE TELEVISION NEWS INTERVIEW
    Akiba A. Cohen
19. UNDERSTANDING VIDEO:
    Applications, Impact, and Theory
    Jarice Hanson
20. EXAMINING NEWSPAPERS:
    What Research Reveals About America's Newspapers
    Gerald Stone

additional titles in preparation

David Pearce Demers
Suzanne Nichols

PRECISION JOURNALISM

A Practical Guide

Volume 15. The Sage CommText Series

SAGE PUBLICATIONS
The Publishers of Professional Social Science
Newbury Park   Beverly Hills   London   New Delhi

For information address:

SAGE Publications, Inc.
2111 West Hillcrest Drive
Newbury Park, California 91320

SAGE Publications Inc.   SAGE Publications Ltd.
275 South Beverly Drive   28 Banner Street
Beverly Hills   London EC1Y 8QE
California 90212   England

SAGE PUBLICATIONS India Pvt. Ltd.
M-32 Market
Greater Kailash I
New Delhi 110 048 India

Printed in the United States of America

Library of Congress Cataloging-in-Publication Data

Demers, David P.
Precision journalism.

(The Sage commtext series ; v. 15)
Bibliography: p.
Includes index.
1. Journalism--Methodology.   I. Nichols, Suzanne.
II. Title.   III. Series.
PN4775.D43   1987   070′.01′8   87-12044
ISBN 0-8039-2946-3
ISBN 0-8039-2947-1 (pbk.)

CONTENTS

PREFACE

Precision Journalism: A Practical Guide is an introduction to the social science research methods used by journalists to gather the news— the survey, including public opinion polls, and content analysis. These methods of reporting are called precision journalism.

This handbook is written for journalism students and working journalists, especially public affairs and investigative reporters, who have had no previous experience with social science research. It is intended to be a straightforward, easy-to-understand explanation about how to use quantitative research methods and how to write about the results.

We wish to express our gratitude to those who helped us in so many ways. Sharon Dunwoody, Gerald Kosicki, and Mary Schaefer of the University of Wisconsin; Simon Dinitz and Richard Lundman of Ohio State University; Richard Carson of the *Columbus Dispatch*; John Schweitzer of Texas Technological University; Chris Moore of Winona Research, Inc.; Norma Steele-Burman of Melon Bank; Michael Norman of *Columbus Monthly*; Guy Meiss, Alan Nichols, Michael Petrick, and Thomas Rood of Central Michigan University, and Cliff Armstrong all read early drafts of parts of the manuscript and offered suggestions and encouragement.

David Ashenfelter and Michael Wagner, special project reporters at the *Detroit Free Press*, were most generous with their off-duty time, telling the story of their investigation of the Michigan Department of Corrections. Their project, which resulted in the six-part series "Revolving Door Prisons," is described in Chapter 10.

Alan Town of the Reporters' Committee for Freedom of the Press and Linda Durling, a former Reporters' Committee intern, provided the information on how to use state and federal Freedom of Information statutes to gain access to public records. Eleanor Myers of the Journalism Department at Central Michigan University, Cathleen Nichols of the Pillsbury Company, Joe Baker of the *Dallas Times Herald*, Mona Rae Pearce Demers, and Alan Nichols all gave assistance and support during the final phases of the project.

We also owe a debt to the American Association for Public Opinion Research, the *Charlotte Observer*, the *Chicago Tribune*, the *Dallas Times Herald*, the *Detroit Free Press*, the *Detroit News*, and the *Wall Street Journal* for granting us permission to reprint extensive excerpts of stories and other materials. Examples from precision journalism projects were also gathered from the *Akron Beacon Journal*, the *Arizona Republic,* the *Columbus Dispatch*, the *Dubuque Telegraph Herald*, the *Indianapolis Star*, the *Miami Herald*, the *Milwaukee Sentinel,* the *Philadelphia Inquirer,* and the *St. Louis Post-Dispatch*. Jeremy Cohen of Stanford University provided a valuable review of an early manuscript.

A special word of thanks also goes to Everette E. Dennis, editor of the Sage CommText Series. All those mentioned here improved the manuscript immeasurably.

All errors, of course, are ours.

1

A METHOD OF INQUIRY

Precision journalism, like conventional reporting, is a method of inquiry—a way of learning about the world.

On its face, it was the kind of commonplace crime Americans have become accustomed to reading about: A man walks into a convenience story in Bay City, Texas, robs the clerk, kidnaps her, rapes her, shoots her with a .45 caliber pistol and leaves her dead on a deserted road.

But nothing about the murder of Loretta Jones was ordinary. The degree of violence was extraordinary. That she was killed by Donald Lee Vigneault was extraordinary. That he was sentenced to die for the crime was extraordinary.

Loretta Jones was black. Her killer was white. That alone made it a relatively unusual murder. The fact that her killer received the death penalty made the case an even greater rarity.

Statistics compiled by the *Times Herald* indicate that whites face odds of roughly one in 17 of being sentenced to death for killing blacks and, so far, virtually no chance of that sentence being carried out. Since the U.S. Supreme Court ended in 1976 what amounted to a four-year ban on executions, 123 blacks have been put to death for killing whites, but no white has been executed for killing a black.

According to FBI records, 2.5 percent of the "capital" murders solved by police agencies between January 1977 and December 1984 involved a white killer and a black victim. But only 1.6 percent of the Death Row inmates whose crimes occurred during that period were whites who murdered blacks.

Conversely, 25.8 percent of the solved "capital" murder and 29.4 percent of the Death Row inmates involved black killers of white victims.

Whites who kill blacks, then, are prosecuted and sent to Death Row in proportionately lower numbers than blacks who kill whites. . . . [1]

This was the beginning of one of the stories in a *Dallas Times Herald* series that reported the results of a nationwide study of capital murder and capital punishment. The reporters obtained information from the Supplementary Homicide Reports of the FBI and rosters of death row inmates from every state that has the death penalty. The data was fed into a computer and 16,173 murders that qualified for capital punishment were analyzed. To determine the race of the victims, the reporters used local policy and sheriff records, medical examiners' records, court documents, and interviews with lawyers, prosecutors, and others familiar with the cases. In some instances, the NAACP Legal Defense Fund and the American Civil Liberties Union provided information on the victims.

WHAT IS PRECISION JOURNALISM?

The *Times Herald* reporters used *precision journalism* along with conventional investigative reporting techniques to uncover the facts for this impressive series. Precision journalism, like conventional reporting, is a method of inquiry—a way of learning about the world. The difference is that *quantitative* social science research methods are used to gather the news. By quantitative, we mean that events, characteristics, behaviors, or attitudes are converted into numbers and then analyzed.

The two major methods of precision journalism are *content analysis* and *survey research*. (A third method, the field experiment, is not treated here.) The first method typically uses documents or records as the cases; the second uses people. The *Times Herald* reporters used content analysis on a variety of local, state, and federal agency records to come up with their conclusions about capital punishment. Other examples:

- Reporters for the *Charlotte Observer* used content analysis on campaign finance reports in North Carolina and found a strong correlation between legislative voting patterns and campaign contributions.
- The *Detroit News* analyzed 35,919 drunk-driving conviction records and found that judges in small towns and rural areas gave stiffer penalties than those in big cities.
- The *Miami Herald* found, after studying property tax records, that the rich were not paying their share of taxes.
- *Akron Beacon Journal* reporters compiled statistics on zoning recommendations and concluded that a local law firm was unusually successful in getting the city council to support its requests.

The survey method involves scientifically sampling and interviewing people to analyze and report what they said. Many news organizations, such as the *Wall Street Journal* and NBC, the *New York Times* and CBS, and the *Washington Post* and ABC jointly sponsor opinion polls, especially at election time. Others use surveys in conjunction with major investigative reporting efforts or to assess public opinion on a number of social and political issues. For example:

- The *Arizona Republic* surveyed Phoenix-area residents and found that the majority believe adults have the right to view sexually explicit movies or video cassettes in private, but not in theaters.
- The *St. Louis Post-Dispatch*, along with KMOX radio, used survey techniques to find that proposals for a Missouri state lottery and horse-track betting enjoyed the solid support of voters.
- The *Dallas Times Herald* surveyed 1,212 passenger airline pilots as part of its extensive "How Safe Are the Skies?" series and found that two-thirds of them believe deregulation has made air travel more dangerous.
- The *Milwaukee Sentinel* surveyed Wisconsin adults about their attitudes toward working women and found that the majority feel that women working is good for the economy and for society as a whole.
- The *Dubuque Telegraph Herald* polled doctors and found that 2 out of 10 have been sued for malpractice and have altered their practice as a result.

THE ORIGINS OF PRECISION JOURNALISM

To some degree, the media have been using precision-journalism techniques for more than 50 years. In 1935 *Fortune* magazine published what is believed to be the first scientific poll conducted by a news organization. Among other things, the survey asked how many cigarettes Americans smoke, what types of cars they intended to buy, and "who favors sharing the wealth" (Felgenhauer, 1971). In 1939, *Reader's Digest* visited auto, watch, and radio repair shops and found that more than half falsely diagnosed or overcharged for repairs. This was perhaps the first example of a field experiment, another research method that can be used for precision-journalism projects. And a few news organizations experimented with public-opinion-polling in the 1950s.

Then came the 1960s and things changed. For one thing, computers became available for social science research, which made data collection and analysis much easier than before. Second, because of the social upheaval of the decade, traditional "objective" journalism came under fire for failing to offer insightful and comprehensive accounts of the world. An "underground press" sprang up. New journalism, advocacy journalism, modern muckraking, and reportage became the vogue. Along with the election poll, some news organizations began using social science research methods to explore social problems. One of the first and best examples came in 1967 when Philip Meyer, a former

Nieman Fellow at Harvard University, supervised a *Detroit Free Press* survey to explore the causes of the Detroit race riots. He subsequently did other projects for the *Miami Herald* and other Knight newspapers for whom he worked as a Washington correspondent.

Two events in 1973 had a profound effect on the use and development of precision journalism. The first was another research project. *Philadelphia Inquirer* reporters Donald Barlett and James Steele designed and executed the first content analysis of court records sponsored by a news organization. They collected more than 100,000 pieces of information on 1,034 defendants charged with violent crimes. With the help of Meyer, the reporters pored through more than 4,000 pages of computer printouts, and found a great deal of disparity in the way defendants of different social and ethnic backgrounds were treated by the criminal justice system. The series won two national journalism awards.

The second event in 1973 was the publication of Meyer's *Precision Journalism: A Reporter's Introduction to Social Research Methods* (Meyer, 1973). The book became a standard reference manual in many newsrooms and advanced reporting classes. It is still widely consulted and contains an excellent discussion of the philosophy, as well as the techniques, of the method.

Meyer originally intended to call the book *The Application of Social Science Methods to the Practice of Journalism*, but when a journalism professor, Everette Dennis, now director of the Gannett Center for Media Studies, suggested he call these methods "precision journalism," Meyer changed his mind. Through the years, the use of social science techniques for news gathering has been called a number of things, including new journalism, computer-assisted journalism, scientific journalism, and quantitative journalism, but none seem as appropriate as precision journalism.

With a new name and a distinct identity, precision journalism finished out the 1970s rather strongly. More than a third of the daily newspapers in the United States had sponsored at least one poll, and more than 80% of them said they would conduct more (Rippey, 1980). Additionally, several schools of journalism instituted courses in precision journalism. One of them, Northwestern University, ran short courses for reporters and editors. Among the teachers of the short courses were Meyer and communication researchers Maxwell McCombs and Kristen McGrath.

Since then, the incidence of polling has remained fairly stable. However, a 1986 study conducted by one of the authors of this text showed that newspapers are relying more heavily on polling experts to handle key aspects of the research process (Demers, 1987). This suggests that the quality of polling by newspapers is improving.

PRECISION JOURNALISM IN PRACTICE

Precision journalism has come a long way since 1935, but it has encountered a great deal of resistance through the years. Some editors and their publishers felt it cost too much or took too much time. Because most news organizations did not have staff trained in research, some were skeptical about its value. This is changing. Journalism schools are turning out qualified researchers and the naysayers can no longer deny the contributions that precision journalism has made to the news business.

Time and money remain concerns, but these too are not the obstacle they used to be. With a basic knowledge of the research process, a personal computer and, say, 100 to 200 hours, a precision journalism project can be undertaken on a variety of topics. For example, students in an introductory reporting class at Ohio State University devised a survey in order to assess student and landlord opinions toward housing costs. The students did the interviewing themselves. The only costs involved were for photocopying, and the project was fielded in less than two weeks. Another group of students investigated police dispatching records to determine whether police response to emergency calls varied across precincts. The data were collected in three days and the entire project took just four weeks to complete. Journalism schools and newspapers may mutually benefit by combining resources to conduct projects.

THE CASE FOR PRECISION JOURNALISM

In late 1976, New York City experienced a major crime wave—at least according to the news media. For seven weeks, newspapers and local television news shows featured stories about crimes committed against the elderly.

Although the incidents themselves were real, the context was not. Police statistics were *not* showing an increase in crimes against the elderly. Yet the impression of a crime wave was created because police were making special efforts to forward reports of such crimes to the news media. Why? Police wanted to generate public support for the plans to allocate more human resources to a special crime-fighting force. Their efforts were successful, partially because the media cooperated (Fishman, 1980: 4-10).

This example illustrates a potential pitfall of conventional reporting—sources using reporters to further their own gain. Although reporters are becoming more and more sophisticated and better equipped to guard against being manipulated by sources, they still must rely heavily on them for their day-to-day news gathering.

A project such as the *Times Herald* series can use precision journalism to offer protection against source manipulation. Instead of relying on a few subjective participants of an event to get the story, reporters systematically examined many individual cases. Criminal court judges, for instance, might say they treat all types of defendants fairly, but a content analysis of court records can show if defendants of different social and ethnic backgrounds are treated equally.

And precision journalism, specifically a public opinion poll, has another appealing quality. It generates news from the average citizen. Most news originates from politicians, government officials, public relations people, prominent citizens, and celebrities. The public often is neglected—there are no "general public" beats. In this same vein, journalists have always prided themselves on being in touch with the public's point of view. Systematic analysis of public opinion is one of the most effective ways to continue and enhance this understanding.

For example, in 1985 the *Los Angeles Times* surveyed both journalists and the public and found that reporters and editors are much more liberal than the general public on a wide range of social and political issues, but that the public did not believe that a liberal bias entered into the news-gathering process.

Finally, precision journalism offers a means of obtaining information not available through conventional news-gathering methods. By using scientific research methods, reporters have been able to identify causes of traffic accidents, determine whether police were slower to respond to citizen complaints in one neighborhood than in others, assess whether a city council favored a developer on rezoning issues, and ascertain whether wealthy property owners were paying their fair share of taxes.

Precision journalism is not a panacea. It does not replace conventional reporting, it supplements it. But whenever there is an interest in describing or explaining the behavior, beliefs, knowledge, or attitudes of some population, group, or other collectivity, precision journalism is an extremely effective methodology.

THE ELEMENTS OF SCIENTIFIC INQUIRY

To use precision journalism, a reporter must learn something about social science research methods. Let us begin by defining scientific inquiry.

First, scientific inquiry must be *logical*, that is, it must make sense. Second, that logic must be supported by observations or *empirical facts*, not hearsay or opinion. Although these criteria may seem simple, living up to them can be quite difficult. That is one reason why researchers follow so many rules.

Scientific inquiry is not the only way to understand the world. Indeed, much of the time casual observation and trial-and-error inquiry work quite well. When we want to know how much money we have in our wallet, we count it. When we want to go on a picnic, we check the weather. And through trial and error, some of us have learned how to use a personal computer. But these methods of inquiry cannot keep pace with a society facing increasingly complex problems. In short, what separates scientific inquiry from everyday casual observation is a careful consideration of logic and empirical facts.

Precision Journalism and Social Science Research

During the research process, precision journalists follow the same rules, guidelines, and procedures that social scientists do, but their approach differs in two ways.

The first is in terms of focus. Precision journalists are concerned with contemporary social and political issues; social scientists are more concerned with isolating general principles associated with human behavior or organization. Explaining factors that always influence voting behavior is a good task for a political scientist; explaining why some people vote for Candidate X is a good task for a precision journalist. On the whole, precision journalists are less likely to be interested in what causes something than in describing it.

The second way in which precision journalism and social science research differs is in terms of the end product. News stories are the outcome of a precision-journalism project. A book or publication in an academic journal is generally the goal of social science research. Journalists, writing for the general public, strive to make complex issues simple, whereas scholars can assume their readers are generally familiar with both the research process and the subject matter.

Descriptive and Explanatory Research

The two basic approaches to scientific inquiry, as we alluded to earlier, are descriptive and explanatory analysis.

Descriptive analysis involves describing a group in terms of its beliefs, attitudes, behaviors, or characteristics. A good example of a descriptive study is the U.S. Census, conducted every 10 years by the federal government. Census workers collect information on the sex, race, age, occupation, and other characteristics of the citizenry. The Census Bureau does not attempt to explain why the population is as it is, it merely describes it. Another example would be a poll that describes how people feel about tax reform.

Explanatory analysis goes one step further. It seeks to account for why something is as it is. At the heart of explanatory analysis is the concept of cause and effect. In the statement "Education has a positive effect on income," education is the cause, income the effect. Explanatory analysis can involve more complex procedures than descriptive analysis, but the payoff can be much greater. It may be useful to know what percentage of the population commits a particular crime—a fact that the descriptive approach will uncover—but the implications are far greater when causes of that crime are determined.

STAGES IN THE RESEARCH PROCESS

Now that we have discussed some of the fundamental characteristics of scientific inquiry, let us briefly turn to an overview of the stages involved in a typical project.

The research process begins with an idea, usually a question or a series of questions. "How are the courts handling rape cases?" "How does the public feel about tax reform?" "Why have there been so many airplane crashes this year?" The same processes that generate day-to-day news are behind precision-journalism projects. The following excerpt from an *Indianapolis Star* story explains why and how one precision journalism project began:

Curiosity as well as alarm prompted an investigation by the *Indianapolis Star* into the high divorce rate in Marion County. It began in May 1984 with a search through court docket books and files for names and addresses and continued with a survey on divorce mailed in November and December 1984 to 1,300 people divorced in Indianapolis in 1983 and 1984.[2]

Although the process of generating a research idea or a daily news story is not complex, ideas do not originate in a vacuum.

First, there must be interest in the topic. That interest will most likely center on an issue the reporter considers important to readers or viewers. A second factor is resources. A reporter may be interested in whether a police crackdown on speeding is decreasing highway deaths, but may lack the time, money, or expertise to investigate the issue. To explain behavior a third factor, theory, is necessary. Theory is an explanation for why something occurs or exists. For example, reporters at the *Charlotte Observer* speculated that campaign contributions would influence the way legislators would vote on an antipollution measure. This hypothesis, or theory, was then tested by comparing the votes of legislators who received contributions to those who did not. (See Chapter 6.) Those involved in a precision-journalism project may borrow from established formal theories or they may engage in their own informal theorizing before they begin investigating the causes of some behavior or phenomenon.

Once the reporters have their ideas and the resources to do the project, they must begin by defining their concepts, developing their hypotheses—if the project involves explanatory research—and deciding which method will work best to gather their data. After this, the project is fielded; in other words, the data are collected. Finally, the findings are written and published.

The remaining chapters in this book address each of these steps. In Chapter 2, we examine how concepts—the fundamental units of observation in research—are created.

NOTES

1. Reprinted with permission of the *Dallas Times Herald*. The story appeared in the *Times Herald* on November 17, 1985.

2. Reprinted with permission of the *Indianapolis Star*. The stories in the series appeared in the *Star* between February 17 and March 3, 1985.

REFERENCES

DEMERS, D.K.P. (1987, forthcoming) "Use of opinion polls as a reporting tool: eight years later." Journalism Quarterly (Winter).

FELGENHAUER, N. (1971) "Precision journalism," pp. 65-75 in E. Dennis (ed.) The Magic Writing Machine: Student Probes of the New Journalism. Eugene: University of Oregon Press.

FISHMAN, M. (1980) Manufacturing the News. Austin: University of Texas Press.

MEYER, P. (1973) Precision Journalism: A Reporter's Introduction to Social Research Methods. Bloomington: Indiana University Press.

RIPPEY, J. (1980) "Use of polls as a reporting tool." Journalism Quarterly (Winter): 642-646, 721.

2

CREATING AND MEASURING REALITY

Concepts are the basic elements of study in precision journalism.

Pornography.

One dictionary calls it "obscene literature or art." Another terms it "writing, pictures, etc., intended primarily to arouse sexual desire." Yet no one, not even the U.S. Supreme Court, has come up with a definition that everyone can accept. This difficulty is illustrated by the 1964 U.S. Supreme Court decision, *Jacobellis* v. *Ohio*. Justice Potter Stewart wrote, "I shall not attempt to further define the kind of materials I understand to be embraced within that shorthand definition; and perhaps I could never succeed in doing so. *But I know it when I see it*" [emphasis added].

If all of us could "see" pornography through Justice Stewart's eyes, the problem of defining it would be resolved. But we cannot, and it is this lack of a specific and precise definition that causes those who want to control the production and distribution of obscene materials so much trouble. To describe, explain, or solve a problem, its concepts must be carefully defined.

CONCEPTS

A concept is an idea, a mental image for an abstraction. Gender, for example, is a concept that represents our mental images of males and females. Attitudes, behaviors, specialized knowledge, and demographics such as education, income, and race are also concepts.

A concept has no intrinsic meaning. It is defined by mutual agreement and can vary over time, cultures, nations, or political systems. Gender, for instance, has no meaning except that which we give it. A visitor from outer space might not be able to *conceptualize* the difference between males and females because, in many respects, they are so alike. Some concepts, of course, are more obvious than others. Concrete objects such as trees, cars, and houses are much easier concepts to understand than are prejudice, hate, jealousy, love, and freedom. Nevertheless, a concept need not be tangible to be studied with quantitative research methods.

Concepts are the basic elements of study and analysis in precision journalism. In descriptive research, they are themselves the topic of interest. In explanatory research, relationships between concepts are studied.

WHAT CONCEPTS ARE STUDIED?

Concepts of the most interest to precision journalists are characteristics, attitudes, beliefs, intentions, and behaviors.

The *characteristics* of a population, called *demographics*, include such things as sex, race, age, income, education, occupation, marital status, and place of residence. Characteristics of an organization, a company, a profession, or an employee group may also be studied.

An *attitude* is a person's positive or negative feelings toward some object or issue: "I like George Bush"; "I am opposed to tax reform"; "I favor capital punishment"; and "I support the new housing development."

A *belief* is what a person thinks about an object or issue: "George Bush would make a good president"; "Tax reform will be bad for the economy"; "Capital punishment deters crime"; and "The new housing development will provide shelter for the poor."

A *behavioral intention* is a predisposition toward performing a particular behavior: "I intend to vote for George Bush"; "I will write my senator about tax reform"; "I will circulate petitions to testify before city council in support of the new housing development."

Behavior, unlike an attitude, can be observed. A reporter can go to court and record the number of times lawyers raise objections and how the judge ruled on those objections. However, behavior is usually measured by asking people to recall what they have done. Even though observing behavior is generally more reliable than relying on someone's memory, it is usually too difficult, too impractical, or too costly to do so. Researchers therefore often must assume people are relatively accurate observers of their own behavior.

DEFINING AND MEASURING CONCEPTS

The process of defining concepts is called *conceptualization* and *measurement*. The first step involves defining a concept in an ideal or perfect state. Often this is quite simple. You might define gender, for example, in terms of the physiological differences between males and females; you might define pornography by its dictionary definition; sex discrimination as the condition that exists when people are denied opportunities because of their ascribed status, or sex. These definitions, which refer to *abstract* or *theoretical* concepts, are meant to capture the true meaning of something.

But note that there is no one right way to define a concept abstractly. Conceptualizing can vary with circumstances and with method of research. For example, instead of defining gender in terms of physiological differences, a social psychologists might define it in terms of a masculinity-femininity continuum.

After a concept is defined, it must be measured in the "real" world. This is called *operationalizing*. The final product of this process is the *measure* or indicator of the abstract concept.

In a survey, for instance, the measure or indicator is a question. If you wanted to measure the concept of age, you probably would ask respondents, "How old are you?" The question is your operational definition of age—your measure of age. As with abstract conceptualization, there is no single way to operationalize a concept. Instead of asking people how old they are, you could examine their birth certificates. The two measures are not likely to yield exactly the same results because some people will understate their age. The birth certificate route may be a more accurate way to measure age, but it is likely to be an impractical one.

Let us take another example—fear of crime. After some thought, you might conclude that fear of crime is a psychological state that produces anxiety or tension in an individual. This is your abstract definition. Now, how are you going to measure it? You might ask, "Is there any area right around here, say, within a mile, where you would be afraid to walk alone at night?" Note that the abstract definition is an ideal one; you assume there is a phenomenon out there called fear of crime and that it can be measured. In this case, you decide to ask people whether they are afraid to walk in their neighborhood at night.

You could take a different approach and ask people if they are more afraid now than they were a year ago that they will become a victim of a crime. Note, though, this operational definition is different. Before, the definition measured fear of crime in the present and near a person's home; this one measures it over time and in all situations. The objective of your research task should guide you to the most suitable operational definition.

Of course, some abstract concepts—pornography is an example—are extremely difficult to measure. Pornography, as is prejudice, sex discrimination, love, and fear, is intangible. It must be defined by people as being so, and for better or worse, their definitions vary considerably. For instance, only a few people would consider Michelangelo's "The Creation of Adam" in the Sistine Chapel obscene, but when an artist's painting of a partially nude woman appeared on the cover of *Newsweek* several years ago, some public schools tore the cover off or banned the magazine from their libraries. Obviously, nudity alone is not sufficient to qualify a picture as pornographic, so what does? And what about written materials? What combination of sentences and words constitutes obscenity?

These questions draw attention to some serious obstacles, but pornography—or some essence of it—can still be studied. One solution is to define it as the public defines it. Various gradations of sexually explicit materials could be shown to people to find the point at which a majority says the materials are obscene. There are still problems with such an approach, but ultimately it could provide a working definition of pornography.

In other situations, journalists are not very concerned with trying to measure precisely the meaning of an abstract concept. Instead, they are interested in how the public feels about it. For example, the *Arizona Republic* surveyed 600 Phoenix residents in the spring of 1985 and found 87% of them agreeing that "adults have a right to view sexually explicit movies or video cassettes in private." In this instance, what is meant by "sexually explicit movies" is not entirely clear, but the approach nevertheless provided a measure of the public's attitudes toward pornography.

MEASUREMENT ERROR

Researchers hope their indicators accurately and precisely measure the nature of the concepts they have abstractly defined. When they do not, the result is *measurement error*—the degree to which the observed or measured values deviate from the actual or true values. In this regard, the validity and the reliability of the concepts must be considered.

Validity

Validity is the extent to which a measure or indicator actually measures what it is intended to measure. In other words, does the operational definition actually measure the abstract concept? The validity of a measure cannot be proved, but the situation is not hopeless.

Through logic and mutual agreement, researchers can arrive at a satisfactory solution. This is called *face validity*, meaning that the operational definition makes sense.

Let us say that a reporter is interested in measuring the abstract concept social class and that level of formal education is used as the indicator or measure of the concept. Although education certainly contributes to social class, using this one measure is likely to result in an incorrect classification of some people. Self-made millionaires who do not have a high school diploma would score low on the measure while janitors and cab drivers with Ph.D.s would score high.

These incorrect classifications impinge upon the validity of the operational definition. In other words, education alone as a measure of social class does not have good face validity. If two additional indicators of social class—income and occupation—were used, the validity of the operational definition would be substantially improved.

As a rule, multiple indicators of concepts enhance validity because they are more sensitive to nuances that exist in attitudes, characteristics, and behaviors. In the example concerning fear of crime, both indicators— fear of crime in one's neighborhood and fear now versus fear a year ago—could have been used. By doing this, three levels of fear are created: fearful in both situations, fearful in one but not the other, and not fearful in either. Before there were just two, fearful versus not fearful. Although the process of creating multiple indicators for concepts can become quite involved, doing so increases the chance that you are measuring what you intend to measure.

Reliability

Reliability is the degree to which a measure, if repeatedly applied to the same people or in the same situation, yields the same result. Reliability is one aspect or component of validity.

If you wish to test the reliability of one your measures of fear of crime, you might conduct two public opinion polls at the same time and, if the measure is reliable, you would find the same, or nearly the same, results.

Intuitively, some measures are more reliable than others. If you ask people their age, you are likely to get the same or nearly the same results every time. But if you ask them how satisfied they are with their job, you are likely to get different answers at different times because satisfaction can fluctuate from day to day and from task to task. The reliability of measures is assessed over time as different researchers find the same or nearly the same results when investigating the same subject.

It should be noted that a measure that is valid is always reliable, but a reliable measure is not always valid. If, for example, you use education as a measure of social class and get consistent results from one research setting to the next, your measure is reliable. However, as a single indicator of the abstract concept social class, it may not be valid.

Systematic and Random Errors

Beyond this, researchers also talk about two different types of measurement error—systematic and random. As a rule, systematic error reduces the validity of a measure and random error affects the reliability. Of the two, systematic error is more serious.

Systematic or nonrandom errors form patterns that bias the results. Let us pick up on our example of age. Because some people are sensitive about their age, they understate it when they are asked how old they are. This creates a pattern. The results for the group as a whole then are likely to indicate that it is younger than it actually is. This affects the validity of the measure. Fortunately, most people tell the truth, so in practice this kind of systematic error does not cause major problems. A bigger problem occurs when a measure has very little face validity or when a poorly worded question is misinterpreted by a large number of people.

Random measurement error, as the term implies, means there is no pattern to the errors—they are random. If men were asked to indicate their wives' income, a few would underestimate and a few would overestimate. But because these errors are random and do not form a pattern, they would cancel each other out. No major problem would result unless large numbers of respondents incorrectly estimated their wives' incomes. If this were the case, the measure would not be too reliable and its validity would suffer as a result. Other common sources of random error include mistakes made by interviewers when recording responses, errors made in converting data for analysis in the computer, and occasional misunderstandings by respondents that do not form a pattern.

VARIABLES AND CONSTANTS

When researchers are into the nitty-gritty of analyzing their data, they usually call their measures variables. A *variable* is a concept that has two or more categories. Gender is a variable because it has two categories—male and female. The categories themselves are also called *attributes*, characteristics that describe the unit of observation. Being female, rich, young, and single are attributes that describe a person and refer to specific categories on the variables sex, income, age, and marital status.

The opposite of a variable is a *constant*. A constant has only one attribute or category; it does not vary. If you ask people if they eat food, everyone would say "yes" because everyone eats. This is a constant; people do not differ in terms of this behavior. But if you ask them what they eat, the answers would vary. Researchers are more interested in variables than in constants because variables point to differences in behavior.

VALUES

For analytical purposes, the categories of a variable are given a number so that the data can be read by a computer. These are called *values*. For example, the two categories for gender—male and female—could be assigned the values 0 and 1, respectively. Note that the values for some variables, such as age, have quantitative differences and can be rank ordered whereas the values for others are qualitative differences. Although females in the example here are given a higher value than males, there is no quantitative difference between the two. The same is true for a number of other variables such as religion, marital status, and race. Differences on these concepts are all qualitative. The values for age, on the other hand, represent quantitative differences—40 is twice as old as 20. Attitudes and behaviors can also take on quantitative differences. More on this later.

CREATING MEASURES

How you go about creating measures depends on the methods you use for your research project. When you use survey research, your measures take the form of questions. As the researcher, you have tremendous control over the information you collect. However, if you are doing a content analysis of public records, your measures will be constructed from the information in the records themselves and you have little control over how the information and potential concepts are measured unless you collect additional data.

Types of Measures

Questions for opinion polls and other survey-research projects are classified as either open-ended or close-ended. A *close-ended question* includes a list of answers and the respondents are asked to select one or more of the options, or *response categories*. Such questions simplify data analysis because the responses are standardized. An example of a close-ended question is this: "Do you favor the proposed zoning ordinance changes?" Respondents would choose from four responses— "favor," "undecided," "oppose," or "don't know." Or, if a more refined measure were needed, "strongly favor" and "strongly oppose" could be added to the list. When designing close-ended questions, you must be careful to provide all the possible answers, with the possible exception of "don't know."

Open-ended questions do not include a set of response categories. Rather, respondents are asked to talk freely about their feelings on a subject. The interviewer records the responses in much the same manner a reporter takes notes during an interview. An example of an open-ended question would be, "Why do you favor capital punishment?"

Although open-ended questions allow respondents more freedom in their answers than do close-ended ones, open-ended questions do have several disadvantages. One is that interviewers sometimes have difficulty keeping up with respondents' comments. Another is that different interviewers interpret responses differently. Further, the answers to open-ended questions can be difficult to categorize.

Creating Categories for Close-Ended Questions

When measuring social characteristics, the categories for close-ended questions are rather self-evident. Sex has two—male and female. Age is expressed in years and may be coded from an open-ended question such as "How old were you on your last birthday?" or a close-ended one, "Which category does your age fall into: 18-30, 31-40, 41-50, or 50 years of age or older?" Income can be recorded in a manner similar to age. The response categories for education may be presented in terms of formal years of education or by the highest level of formal education—grade school, high school, some college, a two-year college or a technical degree, a four-year college degree, postgraduate work, or a postgraduate degree?

When measuring beliefs, attitudes, intentions, or behaviors the options for response categories are less restrictive. To measure an attitude, there can be 3, 5, 7, or 10 response categories. The scale can be anchored with bipolar adjectives, such as favorable-unfavorable; good-bad; strong-weak. The respondents then select a number between the extremes.

Another way would be to use specific adjectives for each response category. To decide, consider what degree of distinction between responses you need and the type of study you are conducting. To see how these two factors play a role, consider three scales that could be used to elicit attitudes toward the following statement: "The United States is spending too much money on defense."

Option 1
Strongly Disagree 0 1 2 3 4 5 6 7 8 9 10 Strongly Agree
Option 2
Strongly Disagree Disagree Undecided Agree Strongly Agree
Option 3
Strongly Disagree −3 −2 −1 0 +1 +1 +3 Strongly Agree

The first option has the most categories and would provide the greatest degree of discrimination. In other words, people with different intensities of agreement are less likely to be lumped into the same category. Of course, in a telephone interview, it would be difficult to explain a 10-point scale. Before presenting the respondent with the belief statement, the interviewer would have to say something like, "On a scale of zero through 10, where zero represents strongly disagree, 10 strongly agree, and 5 neither agree nor disagree, to what extent would you agree or disagree with the following statement?" Additional comments are sometimes used to help clarify the response options available, but many researchers believe that most people cannot conceptually distinguish between gradations this fine on most issues.

The second option, although it contains the fewest number of response categories and may not distinguish as well between respondents in terms of intensity of agreement, is the most popular for telephone surveys. The respondent can more easily understand the categories as the interviewer reads them, and there is less ambiguity as to what each category stands for.

The third option has the advantage of clearly delineating between neutral, negative, and positive agreement. But in a telephone survey it, like the 10-point scale, would be somewhat awkward to explain. In this regard, it is important to remember that misunderstandings concerning the nature of the response categories will affect the reliability of the data.

Another issue to consider when creating response categories is whether to offer "don't know" as an option. Respondents generally are more likely to take a positive or negative stand on an issue if "don't know" is not offered, even though they may still say "don't know," and should be given that option. But if "don't know" is not offered, respondents who get bored or tired do not have an easy out and are more likely to take a stand on the issue. This is important because too many "don't know" responses reduces the usable sample size and thus jeopardizes efforts to make conclusions about the population. On the other hand, if "don't know" is not provided, some respondents will take a stand when they do not have one, which jeopardizes the validity of your findings. The objectives of your research should guide you on this issue.

Finally, we should note that a "don't know" is not the same as "undecided." "Undecided" represents the middle point on a rank-ordered scale between, for example, favor and oppose. "Don't know" means respondents are unfamiliar with the subject they are being asked about.

RULES FOR DESIGNING GOOD MEASURES

Expect to spend a good deal of time developing and refining questions so that they will accurately measure your concepts. What follows are some general rules for doing so.

(1) *Don't reinvent the wheel.* Social science researchers have already investigated many of the topics you might be interested in. Whenever possible, use measures from previously conducted public opinion polls or social science research projects because they have already been carefully scrutinized. Be certain, however, that the questions will indeed measure the concepts you are interested in.

(2) *Be sure terms are used correctly.* For example, many people use the words "robbery" and "burglary" interchangeably. The two, of course, are quite different. Instead of asking people if they have "ever been robbed," be specific: "Have you ever been mugged or had some possession or money taken from you by force or with a threat of force?"

(3) *Keep the questions as short as possible.*

(4) *Don't word questions in the negative.* With a question such as "Do you agree or disagree that the United States should not support the deployment of nuclear missiles in Europe?" respondents are likely to miss the "not."

(5) *As a general rule, provide both sides of an issue in the question.* Asking respondents, "Do you favor legislation that requires a deposit on wine-cooler bottles?" may result in a bias that favors the "favor" position. One might rather ask, "Do you favor or oppose legislation that requires a deposit on wine-cooler bottles?

(6) *Confine questions to a single issue.* A question such as "Do you favor or oppose legislation that requires deposits on wine-cooler bottles and outlaws selling wine coolers in convenience stores?" would be impossible to answer by those who agree with one part but disagree with the other.

(7) *Use simple language.*

(8) *Be specific about the context.* Asking people if they favor capital punishment tells you nothing about the context in which they favor it. Some might think drunken drivers should be put to death whereas others might favor capital punishment only for convicted murderers.

(9) *Always let your colleagues critique your questions; then pretest your questionnaire.* Pretesting is discussed in Chapter 3.

Let us turn now to the methods used by precision journalists to gather their data.

3

OBSERVING THE WORLD

Survey research and content analysis of public records are the two most frequently used precision-journalism methods.

For more than a year, residents of a Columbus, Ohio, neighborhood had been complaining that police were too slow to respond to their emergency calls. They claimed there were not enough patrol cars on duty in their precinct. The police responded that adding more patrols would cost too much and would spur pleas from other neighborhoods for more protection.

Throughout the controversy, neither the police nor the residents presented any facts to support their positions. The residents cited several isolated incidents of slow response time. Police argued that there were just as many police cars on patrol in that neighborhood as there were in any other. What were the facts? Was there a problem?

Four journalism students at Ohio State University used precision journalism to answer these questions. They randomly selected more than 800 police dispatch records for study. They categorized and examined the records by precinct and by day of week.

Their findings, which appeared in a news story in the *Columbus Dispatch*, indicated that police were no slower in the precincts that served the complaining citizens than they were in other precincts.[1] However, the students did find that in all precincts police were significantly slower on Friday and Saturdays than on the other days of the week. The reason: Although the number of patrols on duty was the same each day of the week, the number of complaints was significantly higher on weekends.

This illustrates the importance of looking beyond a few cases to get the whole story. What often appears to be a general pattern is nothing more than isolated events or anomalies. This is where precision journalism can make a difference. Rather than focusing on individual events or behaviors, reporters collect multiple observations before drawing conclusions.

As we noted in Chapter 1, the research methods used most often are survey research and content analysis. Each method has its strengths and weaknesses.

SURVEY RESEARCH

To measure opinions toward some issue or person, journalists use the social survey, commonly called the opinion poll. Some of the more widely known media polls include the *Minneapolis Star and Tribune's* Minnesota Poll, the CBS News-*New York Times* Poll, and the *Los Angeles Times* Poll.

A news organization may work with an outside agency to field the project, or it may use its own staff. The *Detroit News,* for instance, used a research company to conduct a public opinion poll to see if voters felt that race would be an issue in the gubernatorial election. The lead story on September 14, 1986, reported the following:

> Michigan voters say they believe a black can be elected governor, but they aren't convinced that state residents will be color blind when they go to the polls Nov. 4.
>
> At least half think race will influence voters—either for or against Republican William Lucas.
>
> These findings come from the latest *Detroit News* Poll, conducted Sept. 4-7 of 806 registered and likely voters in Michigan. . . .
>
> The poll found that 84 percent believe it is now possible for a black to be elected governor in Michigan, compared with 13 percent who do not.
>
> That attitude is shared about equally by blacks and whites.
>
> Their confidence dims somewhat when asked how race will affect the contest between Gov. James J. Blanchard and Lucas, who is trying to become the nation's first elected black governor. Twenty-six percent say they believe whites will be less likely to vote for Lucas, and 52 percent say blacks will be more likely to support him. . . . [2]

Interviews can be done over the telephone, as they were for the *Detroit News* poll, or at a central location such as a classroom, voting precinct, or a shopping mall. Questionnaires are usually mailed to the respondents' home or office, although they too are sometimes administered in a central location.

Interviewing at a central location is attractive because many respondents can be reached at a relatively low cost, but it should be used only when the entire population is gathered. Exit polling on election day is a good example. The interviewers can be stationed outside of a precinct and survey a sample of voters after they have voted. But note that a shopping mall would not be a suitable place to interview voters before the election because the people there would not likely be representative of all voters. The man-on-the-street poll suffers from the same problem.

Advantages or Disadvantages of Survey Research

The primary appeal of survey research is that generalizations can be made to very large units, such as the population of a city, a state, or an entire nation. However, a major disadvantage is that it is not well suited to the study of complex behavior. A researcher must create measures that all or nearly all of the respondents can understand. This "least-common-denominator" approach means that nuances in attitudes and behaviors are often difficult to measure. Another weakness of the survey is that it assumes people can accurately, honestly, and reliably provide information. Depending on the subject matter, this may or may not be a reasonable assumption.

We should also note the advantages and disadvantages of the three data-gathering techniques most appropriate for survey-research projects: the in-home interview, the telephone interview, and the mail survey.

(1) Response rates. A response rate is the ratio of the total number of interviews to the total number of contacts. Obtaining a high response rate is extremely important. People who refuse to be interviewed or to respond to a written questionnaire may be different from those who do and, as such, the results may not represent the population or the group being studied. When this condition exists, the data is said to be biased.

In-home interviews generally result in the highest response rate. Respondents are less likely to refuse an interviewer standing on their doorstep than they are to hang up the telephone or to throw away a questionnaire they receive in the mail. The mail survey usually produces the lowest response or return rate, especially if the general public is being surveyed. Sometimes a small amount of money or some other incentive is offered to respondents to increase the return rate; but still, there is no guarantee that an adequate level of return will be obtained. The self-administered questionnaire is more practical when the respondents have a special interest in the survey.

(2) Cost. The mail survey is generally the least expensive way to gather data because interviewers will not have to be hired and there are no long-distance telephone bills. The in-home interview is the most

expensive. Sampling, interviewer training, and fielding the project are much more complicated and time-consuming than they are for telephone interviews.

(3) Time. The telephone interview can be completed much more quickly than the in-home interview or mail questionnaire. Note that the interviewing for the *Detroit News* poll was done in four days. This makes the telephone interview extremely attractive to gauge voter opinion just before an election. From startup to data collection, the in-home interview is the most time-consuming.

(4) Interviewer bias. Whenever interviewers are used, there is always the possibility their presence will bias the data. Even when properly trained, interviewers may inadvertently influence responses. A sigh, a laugh, or a nod of approval made at the wrong time may affect the way respondents answer questions. A bias can also stem from other less obvious sources, such as racial, physical, or cultural differences between the interviewer and the respondent. Such differences are less noticeable over the telephone and, of course, nonexistent in a mail survey.

(5) Reaching respondents. A drawback to telephone interviewing is that about 8% of the homes in the United States do not have telephones. Because people without phones tend to be low income, they will be underrepresented in a sample. Although some researchers will weight the data to increase the number of low-income respondents, potential respondents who do not have phones still may differ from those who do.

A list of names and addresses is required to do a mail survey. It is relatively easy to get a voter registration list, but where would you get a list of all working females in the community? Another disadvantage to the self-administered questionnaire is that the respondents must be able to read and write. Samples for in-home interviews of the general public are usually drawn by dividing a community into a number of geographical areas with most residences initially having a chance to be included.

(6) Completeness. It is easier to probe, clarify, and record spontaneous answers during an in-home interview than during a telephone interview. If the personal interview is arranged in advance, as it should be, more information normally can be obtained than from a telephone interview. Generally, a telephone interview should last no longer than 15 minutes, but an in-home interview may last an hour or more. Another advantage of the face-to-face interview is that nonverbal behavior can be recorded.

With self-administered questionnaires it is difficult to get good, insightful results from open-ended questions. Many people do not like to take the time or effort to write their thoughts down. A mail survey also tends to generate more "don't know" and "no answer" responses.

However, in contrast to the interview, the mail survey allows respondents the opportunity to check with others or with their records to verify the accuracy and depth of the information they are giving.

(7) Visual aids. The face-to-face interview permits interviewers to use visual aids such as maps and response boards during the interview. These aids offer an opportunity to probe issues in more depth.

(8) Anonymity. The face-to-face interview offers less assurance than the telephone interview or the self-administered questionnaire that confidentiality will be preserved. Respondents are less likely to be honest and candid if they feel their anonymity is threatened. Some may also feel embarrassed to express their true feelings when an interviewer is present.

(9) Control. A personal interview allows the interviewer to control the questioning, and to know who is answering the questions. There is no guarantee in a mail survey that the appropriate respondent is answering the questions.

Approaching the Respondent

Regardless of whether interviews or self-administered questionnaires are used, you must provide some background information to the respondents before they answer the questions. Introductory statements should include at least four things:

(1) Identification—Interviewers should indicate clearly who is sponsoring the study and, of course, they should identify themselves. A telephone number and an address should be listed on a mail questionnaire and should be given during a telephone interview if requested.

(2) Purpose of the study—In very general terms, the purpose of the study should be given. For example, the interviewers could say, "Today we're interviewing people about their opinions toward candidates in the upcoming election." It is not necessary to be too specific, but interviewers should give the respondents an idea as to why they are being interviewed.

(3) How respondent was chosen—When initially contacted, some respondents feel their privacy has been invaded. This is particularly true when unlisted telephone numbers are drawn through a random-number generation procedure. A brief statement such as "Your telephone number has been randomly selected from all of the telephone numbers in the community" will help alleviate such concerns.

(4) Assure respondent anonymity—The introductory statement must explicitly assure respondents that their comments will be kept confidential. In addition, they should be assured that the purpose of

the interview is not to sell a product or service. "Let me assure you that your comments will be kept in strict confidence and that this is not a sales call" is an example of such a statement.

Constructing the Questionnaire

A questionnaire, of course, is the *instrument* for the survey. Both the wording and the physical design must be clear to ensure that it will be filled out correctly (see Figure 3.1).

The order in which questions are presented can affect responses. If a series of close-ended questions about the fairness of the current tax structure are presented and then some open-ended questions about proposed changes in the tax system, you are likely to get responses related to the close-ended questions. It might be better to switch the order of the questions. Generally, do not ask sensitive or controversial questions at the beginning of the interview before respondents have a chance to feel comfortable. Particularly in a mail survey, it is a good idea to have some interesting questions up front to capture the respondents' interest. And, as a rule, key questions should not be placed at the end of a questionnaire because some people will tire or drop out before they get that far. However, demographic questions such as race and income, which some people feel are sensitive, are usually placed at the end.

Not all questions need to be asked of all respondents. For example, suppose respondents are asked, "Have you ever contributed to an Individual Retirement Account?"

Only those who answer "yes" need to be asked, "Would you contribute again if you were unable to take a tax deduction for that contribution?" The second question, which depends upon the first one, is called a *contingency question*. On the questionnaire, a *skip pattern* is created with arrows directing the interviewer or respondent to proceed to the next question. A skip pattern must be very clearly marked in self-administered questionnaires (see Figure 3.2).

CONTENT ANALYSIS

Content analysis is similar to survey research except that documents, not people, are studied. For precision-journalism projects, content analysis most commonly involves examining the records of various governmental bodies. Indeed, some of the most hard-hitting precision-journalism projects have stemmed from content analyses of such public records.

(Circle the number of your response.)

We hear a lot of talk these days about liberals and conservatives. Below is a seven-point scale on which the political views that people hold are arranged from extremely liberal to extremely conservative. Where would you place yourself on this scale?

(1) Extremely liberal
(2) Liberal
(3) Slightly liberal
(4) Moderate, middel of the road
(5) Slightly conservative
(6) Conservative
(7) Extremely conservative

(Place a check mark next to your response.)
Into which category does your annual family income fall?

_____ Under $20,000
_____ $20,000 to $34,999
_____ $35,000 to $49,999
_____ More than $50,000

Figure 3.1: Examples of Questions for a Self-Administered Survey

Detroit Free Press reporters, for example, examined state Department of Correction records of 5,762 prison inmates paroled in one year. They found errors in nearly 45% of the computerized sentence records and that some of the errors resulted in prisoners being released before their minimum sentence was up. (See Chapter 10 for a more detailed discussion of this project.) And reporters at the *Miami Herald* studied property tax records and found that people who owned more expensive homes were not paying their proportionate share of property taxes. Still another example: The *Dubuque Telegraph Herald* studied police reports of traffic accidents and concluded that police filed fewer charges when someone was injured than when no one was because they were too busy at the accident scene helping the injured to consider who was to blame.

Content analysis is an attractive methodology because it can be relatively easy and inexpensive to collect data. Although the *Free Press* prison project took four reporters and nine months to complete, not all

Have you ever contributed to an Individual Retirement Account?

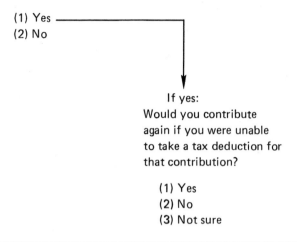

(1) Yes ————————————————┐
(2) No   │
                        ▼
                    If yes:
                    Would you contribute
                    again if you were unable
                    to take a tax deduction for
                    that contribution?

                        (1) Yes
                        (2) No
                        (3) Not sure

Figure 3.2: Skip Pattern

projects do. Other major advantages of content analysis include the following:

(1) Unobtrusive observation—Unlike the survey and the experiment, content analysis does not impose an artificial environment upon the units or cases being studied. The records usually reflect behavior as it occurs in its actual setting.
(2) Changes over time can be studied—Because many public and private records go back many years, you can study long-term changes.
(3) It is easy to collect a large sample—With content analysis, you can relatively easily obtain a large sample because you do not have to depend upon people being home or on them sending questionnaires back. In addition, it is sometimes possible to sample the entire universe, as the *Free Press* did when studying parolees, to eliminate sampling error completely.

A major disadvantage of content analysis, however, is that public records do not always contain all of the information you may need for your project. For instance, traffic accident records typically do not contain the educational and income levels of the drivers involved. If you are interested in analyzing these two variables, you would have to use some other method to get the information.

Another problem journalists sometimes encounter when involved in a content analysis project is gaining access to the data they need. Although most public records are available to the public, the caretakers are often reluctant to allow access, sometimes because of the inconvenience it creates, and sometimes because they fear what the findings may reveal. There is a solution, however, in the provisions of state and federal Freedom of Information statutes.

Gaining Access to Public Records

Under both federal and state Freedom of Information statutes, you have the right to examine and copy governmental records. Although individual state laws differ somewhat in their provisions, the procedures for obtaining access are basically the same whether you are petitioning a state or a federal agency.

First, try an informal approach—call or drop by the department to make your request. Be prepared to pay a reasonable search and copy fee. If your request is denied, file a Freedom of Information request by writing a letter to the public information officer of the department or agency. In the letter, which should be written on letterhead stationery, mention the state or federal act under which you are requesting information, the specific materials you need, and identifying information such as names, places, and periods of time. As a journalist, you may be eligible to have the search and copy fee waived if the information will be used to benefit the general public. Ask. Finally, your letter should indicate that you look forward to hearing from the agency within the time period the act requires— typically 7 to 10 days.

Because all FOI statutes contain certain exemptions from disclosure—such as national security, internal agency rules, trade secrets, investigatory records, and personal privacy—you may not be able to obtain all the information you want. Do not hesitate to negotiate. Make certain the information that is being withheld is truly an exemption under the law.

Note how David Ashenfelter handled his request to the Michigan Department of Corrections when he petitioned for the prison records he needed for the *Free Press* series:

Public Information Officer
Michigan Department of Corrections
P.O. Box 30003
Lansing, MI 48909

Dear ————:

This is a request under the Michigan Freedom of Information Act. I would like to obtain current copies of computer tapes from the following MIS files: Master file, Identification file, Sentence Data file, Movement file, Orders for Parole file, and Parole Board Action file.

I've attached a list of data I would like included on each file. If you feel any of the information I am requesting is exempt from disclosure under the FOIA, please contact me by telephone so we may resolve any such problems as quickly as possible.

Before processing this request, please provide me with an estimate of how much each file will cost.

Depending upon the duplication fees, I may wish to defer my request for some files until a later date.

Thanks in advance for your assistance.

Sincerely,
David L. Ashenfelter

If your request is denied, you should appeal to the head of the agency by writing a brief letter saying why you believe the denial was improper and requesting a review. Attach copies of all correspondence. If that does not work, you have the right to file an FOIA lawsuit. You may want to contact the Reporters Committee for Freedom of the Press for advice. The committee's address is 800 18th Street, NW, Washington, DC 20006.

Recording Data for Content Analysis

Although you will not be using a questionnaire when doing a content analysis, you will need some sort of a form to record the information in the records. The information recorded on this *coding sheet* later will be entered into a computer. The design of the coding sheet will depend upon the records you are examining. We recommend that a separate sheet be used for each record.

Analysis of Nonpublic Records

Content analysis may also be used to examine documents other than public records. For example, newspapers could be categorized in terms of their political orientation, geographic location, and size to see what effects these variables have on political candidate endorsements. Generally, though, reporters find public records an inexhaustible source of data.

RESEARCH DESIGN

Whichever research method you decide to use, you must also decide how to handle a number of other key issues. Who will be interviewed? Can the questions be answered with a single study or are two or more studies, conducted at different times, required? If more than one survey is necessary, should the original respondents be recontacted? What kind of sampling procedure should be used? How many people or elements should be examined?

These questions fall under the rubric of *research design*. Although often used synonymously, methodology and research design are different. The former refers to the general orientation or approach, whereas the latter examines specific issues within each of the general approaches.

Cross-Sectional Versus Longitudinal Designs

A *cross-sectional* study is used to find out how a group feels about something or someone today. But if you are interested in how opinions change over time, then a *longitudinal* design or tracking study is more appropriate.

The news media are more apt to rely on cross-sectional surveys because a longitudinal study requires a greater commitment of time and resources. Increasingly, though, researchers are turning to longitudinal designs because of their increased power in investigating cause-and-effect relationships. For example, the effects of a television advertising campaign are assessed much more effectively by conducting a study before and after the advertising begins rather than just after.

Three options are available in longitudinal design—the trend, the panel, and the cohort study. The trend is the most widely used. It involves examining changes in a general population over time. The survey population is defined on some general parameter, such as registered voters in the United States, and subsequent surveys draw new samples from this population. Note that the survey population changes.

The panel study, in contrast, examines the same respondents over time. A group of voters might be reinterviewed every two weeks before an election. This technique has the advantage of detecting minute changes in behavior and attitudes. However, it is often difficult to locate all of the original respondents. And as the sample size dwindles, it becomes more difficult to generalize the findings.

The cohort study borrows characteristics from both the trend and panel study. The same types of people are examined but not the same people. Generally, a cohort is defined as an age group. For example, a population might be defined as everyone born in the 1960s and samples from that group drawn every five years to study how the cohort changes.

Control Groups

Although most commonly associated with laboratory experiments, control groups also may be used in survey research and content analysis. For example, since the late 1970s a number of states have passed laws requiring a mandatory prison sentence if a gun is used during the commission of a felony. To determine whether these laws are successful in reducing crime rates, researchers could examine the crime rates in states that have passed the laws, as well as those that have not. By doing so, they could control extraneous factors, such as changing social conditions, to rule out the possibility that they are responsible for differences in crime rates.

Sampling Design

Sampling is another aspect of research design. But because of the important role it plays in the research process, we have devoted the next chapter to it.

NOTES

1. The story appeared May 17, 1981.
2. Used with permission of the *Detroit News*. The story appeared on September 14, 1986.

4

SELECTING CASES FOR STUDY

Generalizations about very large populations can be made from a small number of cases when probability-sampling methods are used.

In the days just preceding the 1976 presidential election, Gerald Ford and Jimmy Carter were running neck and neck in the polls. They were so close, in fact, that most pollsters were unwilling to predict who would win. There was one exception.

Pollster Burns Roper said Carter would win. His final poll showed Carter leading Ford 51% to 47%. This came within one percentage point of the final result.

Quoted later by the Associated Press, Roper said, "Polling is part science and a helluva lot of human judgments. Fortunately, we made the right ones." In the same vein, George Gallup, another famous pollster, remarked: "The plain fact of the matter is that you have to be lucky. You have to repeal the laws of probability."

Two years later these remarks ended up in an introductory reporting textbook, under the heading: "Luck as a Factor." To have predicted the 1976 election when a poll indicates no significant difference between two candidates would be, in fact, pure luck, although one would have a 50% chance of being right. But Roper's and Gallup's comments should not be misinterpreted. Luck is not a factor in determining the accuracy of a poll. If it were, polling would not have the track record it does. Except for the 1976 presidential election, when the results were too close to call for most pollsters, national polls have correctly predicted the winner in every presidential election since 1948. The odds of this happening by chance are one in 500.

But what if a poll does not accurately predict the outcome of an election, as was the case in 1948 when Truman won but virtually every poll in the nation predicted that Dewey would win by a landslide? Were the polls wrong? Not necessarily—at least not at the time they were taken. Some voters changed their minds, some who were expected to vote did not; and some who were not expected to go to the polls did.

When sound sampling procedures and good measures are used, a wrong prediction most likely means that public opinion changed after the poll was taken or that people did not follow through on their intentions to vote or to vote for the candidate they said they preferred.

But what are sound sampling procedures? They are the subject of this chapter.

THE UNIT OF ANALYSIS

Determining who or what is going to be studied—the *unit of analysis*—is the first step in selecting cases for study. It will be individuals, groups, or documents.

With survey research, the unit of analysis is most often the individual. A public opinion poll, for instance, collects information on attitudes, behaviors, and the personal characteristics of individuals. But instead of individuals, groups can be the unit of analysis. A reporter, for instance, might examine families, cities, states, ethnic groups, census blocks, community groups, political organizations, or corporations. Although information about the group may be obtained from individuals, the characteristics or behaviors examined are those for the group, not the individual.

For content-analysis projects, the unit of analysis is the records of the courts, police, administrative agencies, or legislative bodies, as well as books, newspaper articles, and television commercials.

DEFINING THE POPULATION

After determining who or what will be the unit of analysis, the *population* must be defined. Population as used here does not refer to the population, say, of the United States, but rather to the group or elements about which you are planning to make your generalizations. If you are interested in teachers' perceptions of the educational system, for example, you might define your population as all the teachers currently teaching in private or public K-12 schools in your community. If you want to study personnel policies of the major employers in your community, you might define your population as all companies and organizations that employ more than 50 people. In most national public opinion polls, the population is defined as all persons 18 or older.

This definition of population is the *target population*, or ideal population. It does not take into account the practical limitations of contacting people. At the time of interviewing, some people may be ill, some may not have a telephone, others will be in the process of moving, or on vacation, or maybe even in jail. Because not everyone in the sample is available, the population from which the cases are drawn is referred to as the *survey population*. The validity of the findings, of course, is a function of the degree to which the survey population matches the target population.

Once a population is defined, you decide whether to study all of it or a sample. Studying the entire population is better, of course, because unlike a sample there is no sampling error associated with the observations. *Sampling error* represents the degree to which the results obtained from a sample vary from the actual or true population results. Sampling error is one type of measurement error.

Even though studying the entire population is more accurate than studying a sample, it usually is not very practical. Seldom is there the time and money to interview every adult in the United States or even every one of them in a small community. Fortunately, it is not necessary. Properly drawn samples provide fairly precise estimates of a population.

PROBABILITY THEORY IN SAMPLING

A sample will represent a population if each member or unit of that population is given an equal chance of being included in the sample. This is called a *simple random sample* because there is no order or pattern to the selection of its members. With simple random sampling, findings can be generalized to the entire population within a certain margin of error.

The logic behind how a sample represents a population can be demonstrated by imagining a huge barrel of marbles, one-third red, one-third blue, and one-third green. If you select 300 marbles at random you would expect to have about 100 marbles of each color. Of course, every time you select 300 marbles you will not get 100 of each color, but you will be close most of the time. The degree to which the percentage of each color varies from its percentage in the actual population represents sampling error, which can be estimated using the law of probability.

ESTIMATING SAMPLING ERROR

To understand the principle of sampling error, let us first look at an example that has no sampling error. Assume for the moment that the population you wish to study is all of the students in your classroom or all of the reporters in your newsroom. Since there probably are not too many of them, you ask everyone, "Do you favor or oppose a ban on nuclear or atomic bomb tests?" By doing this, you will discover the population *parameter*—the percentage who favor and the percentage who oppose a ban. Suppose that half say they are in favor of a ban and the other half say they oppose one. Naturally, there is no sampling error because you have interviewed everyone in the population. Of course, the population as defined here refers only to your colleagues, not to the general population.

Now select a sample to see how accurate sampling can be. Since you have to give each member of the population an equal chance to be selected in order to estimate the sampling error, write the name of each person on a piece of paper and put it into the proverbial hat. Blindfolded, select one-fourth of the names and ask these people how they feel about the nuclear test-ban issue. After tallying the results, you find 54% favor and 46% oppose. but your poll or sample results do not precisely match those of the population. You have a 4% difference, which represents the sampling error. You know precisely what the sampling error is because you know the population parameters.

Now, put all the names back into the hat and draw another sample of one-fourth of your colleagues. This time the result is closer—48% favor and 52% oppose—but it is in the opposite direction of the first sample. Take another sample. This time the result is 51% and 49%. Try another: 52% and 48%. Another: 47% and 53%. And another: 49% and 51%. If you continue to take samples and average the results, your average, or mean, would equal the actual population parameter—50% and 50%. If the results of an infinite number of samples drawn from this same population were plotted, they would look like a bell-shaped curve (see Figure 4.1). This is known as the *sampling distribution of the mean*. As you can see, most of the sample results are closely grouped around the population parameter of the 50% you found when you surveyed everyone.

One of the major factors influencing sample error is sample size. The larger the sample, the smaller the sampling error. The bell curve would get taller in the middle and shorter on the ends as the sample size increases. However, sampling error decreases at a slower rate as the sample size increases, as Figure 4.2 shows. Although doubling a sample of 100 results in a large drop in sampling error, doubling a sample of 1,000 results in a very small one. For this reason, public opinion polls usually survey no more than 1,500 to 1,600 people. To interview more just increases the cost of the project—it does not appreciably reduce the

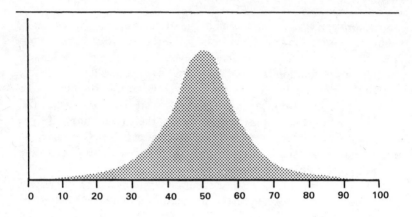

Percent in Favor of a Nuclear Test Ban

Figure 4.1: Sampling Distribution of the Mean

sampling error. It should be noted that as a rule it does not matter how large the population is. Sampling error is the same whether there are 50,000 or 10 billion in the population. Only when the number sampled represents about 5% or more of the population does the size of the sample begin to have an impact on sampling error.

Sampling error is also a function of the degree of difference between elements in the population. The error is greatest when two categories are evenly split—50% and 50%—and lowest when there is wide disparity, say 95% and 5%. Additional comments about sampling error and the formula to calculate it can be found in Chapter 8.

Quality, Not Quantity

In probability sampling, quality—or randomness—is far more important than quantity. Consider what happened in 1936 when the *Literary Digest* incorrectly predicted a crushing defeat for Franklin Roosevelt. The prediction was based on a sample of 2 million people—one of every five voters in the United States. (There were approximately 10 million voters in the United States in 1936.) The sample was drawn from the magazine's subscription list, automobile registrations, and telephone directories. But this was during the Great Depression, and voters who could afford to subscribe to magazines, own a car, or even

Sampling Error

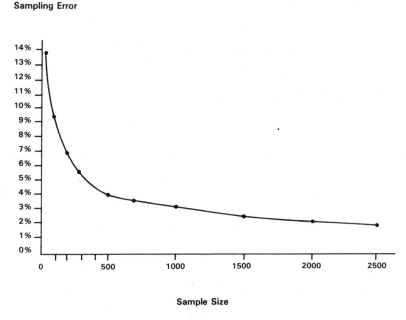

Sample Size

NOTE: Based on a 95% level of confidence. (See Chapter 8 and Appendix B for more information about sampling error and levels of confidence.)

Figure 4.2: Sampling Error for Different Size Samples

have a telephone were those most likely to vote for the Republican candidate.

To be sure, the *Literary Digest* will not be the last to make such errors. A more recent example stems from a 1985 Ann Landers column. She asked her readers to respond to the question, "Would you be content to be held close and treated tenderly and forget about the 'act'?" More than 100,000 women responded and 72% said "yes." Landers concluded that "a great many women choose affection over sex." Although this may be true, the survey provides no basis for making such a generalization about all American women. More likely than not, the women who responded were sympathetic to the purpose of the survey, just as those who owned automobiles in 1936 were more likely to be Republican.

SAMPLING DESIGNS

The simple random sample is the classic probability sampling design, but it is sometimes difficult to conduct. With the exception of populations contained in public records, researchers frequently do not have a complete list of all the elements of a population. In other words, there is no *sampling frame* that contains the names of all the people or cases in the population. Therefore, many surveys and content-analysis projects rely on some other form of sampling.

Stratified Simple Random Sampling

Stratified simple random sampling involves dividing the population into two or more subgroups and extracting a separate sample from each. For example, the United States could be divided into 20 regions. The number of interviews in each region would be in proportion to that region's percentage contribution to the total population. If a region contained 5% of the total population, then 5% of the people interviewed would be from that region. This is called *proportionate* stratified random sampling.

Stratification can be done on a number of variables, as long as you know the population parameters. For this reason, the variables used are usually those found in the U.S. Census. Geographic region, age, and sex are the ones most commonly used.

The primary advantage of proportionate stratified random sampling is that generally it has less sampling error than a simple random sample; at the very least, it will have no more. To illustrate, assume you want to stratify by sex. Because the proportion of males and females you sample will precisely reflect their proportion in the population, there is no sampling error on that variable. In a simple random sample, it is unlikely that the proportion of males and females in a sample will be exactly as they are in the population. This does not mean there is no sampling error in a proportionate stratified random sample, only that there will be none on the stratified variable. Stratification procedures are usually used to control for sampling error on variables that play an important role in the study.

Cluster Sampling

As with stratified sampling, *cluster sampling* involves dividing the population into two or more subgroups. But instead of sampling from all of the subgroups, only some are used. With this technique, a survey might be administered to a sample of adults in 10 of 20 regions of the United States. Cluster sampling, of course, can increase the amount of sampling error because some subgroups, or clusters, are not sampled. In fact, cluster sampling is subject to two sampling errors—one at the point the clusters are sampled and the other at the point cases are selected for each cluster. The error can be minimized by creating clusters that are very similar to each other. The more similar the clusters, the less the variation and the less likely the sample is to contain divergent elements. But this is not always possible. We should also add that estimating the error in a cluster sample can be very complicated.

Despite this drawback, clustering is sometimes the only way to select a sample efficiently. If, for example, a list of people or households is not available, a community could be divided into census blocks, and a sample of the census blocks drawn. Then, within each block, certain homes would be chosen to be included in the sample. A major benefit of this approach is that interviewers would not have to travel all over town to do their interviewing. Cluster sampling is usually used for exit polling. The selection process generally includes a stratification procedure to ensure that all socioeconomic areas of the city are represented. National samples that require in-home interviews generally are drawn using a combination of clustering and stratifying procedures.

Systematic Simple Random Sampling

Systematic simple random samples involve arraying all of the elements of a population and choosing every Nth one. For example, if you want to interview 100 people from a population of 1,000, you would select every tenth name beginning with a random start. Samples drawn from voter registration or association membership lists are often selected this way. Drawing a systematic random sample is usually less time consuming than drawing a random sample, but watch for patterns in the list that could bias the sample. If every even-numbered name on a list is a male and every odd-numbered one is a female and you select every tenth name beginning with an even number, no females will be in your sample.

RESPONSE RATES

Regardless of sample design, the most important criterion for selecting a sample is that it represent its population. Obtaining a high response rate is vital for this because people who refuse to be interviewed may be different from those who do, and you have no way of knowing how they are different. If the number of refusals is high, little confidence can be placed in your findings.

The *response rate* is the number of completed interviews divided by the total number of contacts. Thus if you contact 1,000 people and interview 700, the response rate is 70%. The number of contacts usually includes—in addition to the number of completed interviews—refusals, those who are not available because of illness, those who do not speak English, those who are not home after a specified number of calls, and those who cannot hear or understand the interviewer. Nonworking telephone numbers and noneligible contacts such as business numbers and households where no eligible respondent is available are not included.

No universal standard has been set to define an appropriate response rate, but most researchers believe 50% is acceptable; 60% is good; and 70% or higher is very good. Telephone surveys that employ five or more callbacks generally obtain a 60% response rate. Mail surveys, on the other hand, typically generate a return rate of less than 35%, unless those sampled have a keen interest in the subject matter of the survey. In that case, the return rate for a mail survey can be quite high.

DRAWING A SAMPLE

Drawing a sample need not be difficult. For example, if the population is defined as the total number of registered voters in the county, the sampling frame is available at the county clerk's or election office. For a fee, some of these offices will generate a random sample for you. If you are doing a content analysis of public records, the sampling frame is held by the governmental office or agency. You could elect to sample the records or examine them all if it would not be too time consuming.

If a sampling frame is not readily available—as would be the case if a public opinion poll required the opinions of nonregistered as well as registered voters—other techniques are available. One of the easiest is to select names randomly from a telephone directory. This procedure has a drawback, however. About one-fifth of all working residential telephone numbers in the United States are unlisted. Because socioeconomically upscale people are most likely to have unlisted telephone numbers, they are likely to be underrepresented if a telephone book is used as the sampling frame. To overcome this obstacle, random-digit dialing is often used. With this procedure, all possible area codes, prefixes, and suffixes in an area are listed and numbers are randomly generated by a computer. (See Appendix A.)

For a 50% response rate, at least 10 times as many numbers as the size of the sample should be generated because only about one of every five numbers will be a working residential number. The rest will be unassigned or business numbers. The sample should be as large as possible, but need not be larger than 1,500. As we explained earlier, drawing samples larger than 1,500 results in only minute reductions in sampling error. Unless you want to examine and compare subgroups, the additional cases will cost a lot but will not greatly enhance the generalizability of the data.

Who Should Be Interviewed?

A final issue involved in telephone sampling is who in the household should be interviewed. If the person who answers the telephone is always the one interviewed, the sample is likely to contain a disproportionate number of children and women and thus not be very representative of the general population. To ensure proper representation of both sexes, the last digit of the telephone number can be used to indicate the sex of the person to be interviewed—if the number is even, for example, the male heads of household would be selected; if odd, the female. When the number is even and a household does not contain a male, an interview still may be conducted with the female head of household. To compensate for the fact that single people will have a greater chance of being interviewed than married people, you can *weight* the data or *stratify* by household composition, using census data.

Weighting is a statistical procedure used to balance a sample when a category is over- or underrepresented. To see how weighting works, assume that census data indicate that in your area 35% of the heads of households are single and 65% are married; but in your sample of 1,000, 500 are single and 500 are married. To correct for this over- and underrepresentation, you could weight the responses of each group. First, obtain the weight factors:

$$\frac{\text{Category Share of Population}}{\text{Category Share of Sample}} = \text{Weight Factor}$$

Thus one would get the following for the singles: $350/500 = .70$. For the married respondents the result is: $650/500 = 1.30$.

Let us assume that 500, or 50%, of your sample of 1,000 say that health care is "very adequate." But when you look at the responses by category, you find that 300, or 60%, of the marrieds and only 200, or 40%, of the singles say it is "very adequate." To see then what the impact of the overrepresentation of singles has on the total, you multiply the 200 responses of the singles by .70 and the 300 responses of marrieds by 1.30: 200 × .70 = 140; 300 × 1.30 = 390. Now you have 530 responses of "very adequate" and you would report that 53% say health care is very adequate in your community.

If, instead of weighting the data, you choose to stratify by household composition, you would simply stop calling single heads of house after you had interviewed 350, or 35%, of them. You would continue interviewing married respondents until you had reached your sample size of 1,000.

SAMPLING FROM PUBLIC RECORDS

One of the attractive features of public records is that in most cases you can draw a random sample because the entire population of cases is available. In many instances, a systematic random sample will work very well. If this is not practical, stratification procedures can be used based upon how the records are categorized. For example, the college students who analyzed police records in Columbus did not want to select every Nth case because dispatch records for different precincts varied greatly from day to day and from season to season. To correct for this, they drew a random sample of 21 days out of the year, stratified by day of the week. Then all of the records for each precinct were examined for each of these days.

NONPROBABILITY SAMPLING

It is not always necessary to draw a probability sample in order to make inferences about a population. Cognitive psychologists, for example, study memory processes of college students and still generalize to a larger population because it is reasonable to assume that memory processes, as distinguished from memory, do not vary greatly from person to person.

When the issue involves attitudes and behaviors, though, seldom can a nonprobability sample be generalized to a larger population. This does not mean social scientists never draw nonprobability samples—they do, especially when they are exploring a new topic. But the conclusions from such studies are limited to the respondents sampled. Generalizations to a population can only be made after the same study is conducted on a probability sample from the entire population. Also note that sampling error cannot be calculated for nonprobability samples because the laws of probability do not apply. Precision journalists rarely use nonprobability sampling techniques.

ANALYSIS OF SECONDARY DATA

Throughout this chapter, we have discussed ways to collect *primary* data; that is, data collected expressly for the precision journalism project. But data collected by others, referred to as *secondary data*, can also be used for precision-journalism projects. Consider, for example, the following:

Shortly after President Reagan was wounded in March 1981, reporters for the Cox newspapers did an investigation to determine what types of guns were used in the commission of crimes and who made them. They obtained a computer tape from the U.S. Treasury that detailed the types of guns most often used in violent crimes and found they were the types most easily concealed.

Both the *Fort Lauderdale News and Sun Sentinel* and the *Detroit Free Press* have examined public records to investigate health-care issues.

In 1984 the *News and Sun Sentinel* published a four-part series documenting, among other things, that 20% of heart surgery deaths in Veterans Administration hospitals were due to medical errors and that the VA worked hard to cover up the mistakes. The series was the result of a four-year legal battle between the VA and the *News/Sentinel* over access to VA medical, caseload, and mortality data.

In 1986 the *Free Press* reported the results of its Washington bureau staff's analysis of 1984 federal Medicare records. The reporters found that 44 hospitals had death rates for Medicare patients undergoing coronary bypass surgery that were at least two times higher than the national average.

There are a number of secondary sources of data. The local office of the U.S. Bureau of the Census is a tremendous resource. Some academic institutions are also repositories for data sets collected by government and private researchers. One of the most extensive collections is held by the Inter-University Consortium for Political and Social Research at the University of Michigan. Many of the data sets are available for no cost or for a small fee and can be accessed through a remote computer terminal and a phone line. Another widely used data set is the General Social Survey, a national public opinion poll regularly conducted by the National Opinion Research Center at the University of Chicago. This data base is available at many universities.

In some cases, such as with the VA and Medicare stories, using secondary sources is the only way to get the story. In others, using them saves a great deal of time and money; however, always check the quality of the research design to make sure it is adequate for your purposes.

"FIELDING THE PROJECT"

Once the questionnaire has been designed and the method of collecting data decided, the project is ready to be fielded.

Because of the complexities of in-home surveys and the extensive training interviewers must have, most news gathering organizations hire market research companies, academic researchers, or public opinion polling companies to do data collection; but a telephone poll is easily handled by a news staff.

Still, a number of details must be attended to: obtaining access to telephone facilities, making copies of the questionnaire, hiring and training interviewers, pretesting the instrument, and validating the results.

Training Interviewers

A crucial step in preparing to field a telephone survey is to train interviewers properly. A briefing will be required, during which the questionnaire is read and other key issues discussed. Naturally, it is important that the interviewers be instructed on how to remain neutral, unbiased observers. Although this does not mean they should respond coldly or staidly to jokes and other comments made by respondents, they must not assist the respondent in choosing an answer. Questions should be read verbatim from the questionnaire, and when clarification is necessary, the question should be repeated—interviewers should not attempt to interpret the question for the respondent. Interpretation on the part of interviewers takes the standardization out of a question, creating in essence, a different question. Interviewers should never comment, either favorably or unfavorably, on a respondent's answer—to do so may influence the way other questions are answered. Interviewers should be cordial, friendly, helpful, but detached and professional.

Pretesting the Instrument

Before fielding a project, the questionnaire must be pretested. This allows interviewers to become acquainted with the questionnaire and the interviewing process and helps researchers uncover unexpected problems. Usually 20 or 30 interviews are enough for an adequate pretest. Interviewers should be instructed to record any problems respondents might have answering questions. If necessary, the questionnaire can then be modified before the entire project is fielded.

Keeping Response Rates Up

Some people refuse to be interviewed over the telephone and some are hard of hearing, senile, or cannot speak English. But, you still can have some control over your response rates. One way is to reduce the number of calls classified as "no one at home." If there is no response on the first try, try again and again. The callbacks should be made at different times of the day and on different days of the week. Of course, at some point, you have to concede that it does not make sense to continue calling a number, but we recommend at least five tries. If you are using an outside company to field your project, make sure callbacks are part of the contract. Many private research companies use three callbacks because it reduces their costs, but their response rates are often less than 50%, not acceptable for most precision-journalism projects.

Validating the Results

After the interviews are complete, you need to *validate* the results by calling a random sample of respondents to confirm they were actually interviewed. There are two reasons for this. One is to ensure that the data are reliable because occasionally interviewers, when working under a tight deadline, will fabricate interviews. Of course, interviewers should be told before a project begins that their work will be checked. The second reason to call respondents back is to get some additional feedback so that future surveys can be improved.

Once the data are collected, they must be prepared for analysis—the topic of Chapter 5.

5

DESCRIBING THE WORLD

Descriptive statistics, such as the percentage and mean, summarize and describe data.

> Latins are seven times more likely than Anglos, and nearly three times more likely than American blacks, to be murdered in Miami. . . . And among the city's 1981 slayings, Latins were identified by police as the killers 13 times more often than were nonhispanic whites, and more than twice as often as American blacks.[1]

The *Miami Herald* story went on to provide more details: 141 Latins were killed, compared to 50 blacks and 19 whites; 126 Latins were charged with murder, compared to 60 blacks and 10 whites.

On the surface, the story seems airtight. But look again.

When the per capita victim and offender rates are examined instead of the raw numbers, a completely different picture emerges. For every 100,000 Miami Latin residents, 61 were victims; for every 100,000 black residents, 70 were victims; for every 100,000 white residents, 27 were victims. The offender rate followed the same pattern. There were more Latin victims because there were more Latins; in fact, they make up more than half of the city's population.

As this case illustrates, to avoid analytical errors when working on a precision-journalism project, you must learn how to use and interpret statistics correctly. But, first, let us look at how to collect and prepare the data that is to be analyzed.

PREPARING DATA

A basic knowledge of computers and statistical software is necessary for most precision-journalism projects, but access to a mainframe computer is not necessary. A personal computer can handle nearly all of the needs of a precision journalist. And the variety of easy-to-use data base and statistical software packages available make the task of arranging and analyzing data quite simple.

Coding Data

The first step in the process is coding the data. To do this, you assign a number to each response category so that the computer can read it. For close-ended questions, this can be done before the questionnaire is administered. In fact, the numbers are often on the questionnaire itself to save time at the coding stage. But for open-ended questions, answers must be analyzed after the data is collected and then grouped into discrete categories before numbers are assigned.

The values are then arranged in a data *matrix* (see Figure 5.1). The columns correspond to the variables and the rows to the respondents or cases. For a variable with no more than 10 response categories, only one column is needed, but when there are more than 10 categories, two or more columns are needed to define the measure. Identifying a respondent's sex, for instance, takes only one column but age takes two. Usually the first set of columns is used to identify the respondents and for other background information such as the date of the interview, the respondent's telephone number, and the interviewer. Substantive information then follows.

The Code Book

To keep track of what the numbers mean, you will need to create a *code book* that lists the variables, the column codes, the questions, and the response category codes.

Variables. Before the data can be manipulated, each variable must be identified by name or number. It is less confusing to use the actual name of the variable—sex, age, income, education. But because some software packages limit the number of characters that can be used, you may need to number the variables consecutively—V001, V002, V003.

Column codes. For each variable, the column number or numbers in the data matrix are specified.

Questions. The question or questions used to create each variable are included for reference purposes.

Response category codes. The number assigned to each response category or answer is then listed. For example, if the variable is marital status, 1 would equal single; 2, married; 3, divorced; 4, separated; and 5, widowed. An example of a codebook is provided in Figure 5.2.

Missing Data

When a respondent does not answer a question or when a particular case lacks a specific piece of information, the result is *missing data*—the

					Variables							
Respondent	1	2	3	4	5	6	7	8*	9	10	11	12 ...
1	4	2	5	4	7	5	8	0	2	1	4	3
2	2	5	3	5	1	2	1	1	3	5	4	2
3	2	3	1	4	5	3	4	1	4	3	4	2
4	2	3	1	5	5	6	6	0	2	4	3	3
5	1	4	3	4	3	5	3	1	3	2	3	2
6	3	4	2	8	3	7	3	1	2	4	2	3
7	2	1	5	7	2	3	2	0	5	3	3	2

*Column 8 here is used for the variable Sex. Male = 0, female = 1.

Figure 5.1: Data Matrix

respondent or case is excluded from the analysis. A "don't know" is not the same as missing data, by the way, although sometimes it is recorded as such. With some statistical packages, the column can just be left blank; with others, a code number must be used to indicate that the data is missing.

USING STATISTICS

Once the data is coded and entered into the computer, it is ready to be analyzed. *Descriptive statistics* are used to summarize and characterize data for all types of quantitative research, whether it was collected from a population or from a sample, or whether descriptive or explanatory analysis is being undertaken.

Inferential statistics, on the other hand, are used only when the data are collected from a probability sample. Inferential statistics help researchers determine whether differences observed in data exist in the population or whether they occurred by chance because of sampling error. In this chapter we deal only with those used in univariate, or one variable, descriptive analysis.

Levels of Measurement

First, though, let us consider levels of measurement. Before selecting a statistic to describe or explain your data, you must consider the level at which it is measured because some statistics can be used only with

Column Code	Question	Variable	Responses and Codes
1-4	—	I. D.	Respondent number
5	1	Sex	0 = Male 1 = Female
6-7	2	Age	In years
8	3	Residence	1 = Country 2 = Farm 3 = Small city 4 = Medium city 5 = Suburb 6 = Large city
9-10	4	Education	In years
11	5	Race	1 = White 2 = Black 3 = Hispanic 4 = Asian 5 = Native American 6 = Other
12	6	Politics	1 = Extremely liberal 2 = Liberal 3 = Slightly liberal 4 = Middle of the road 5 = Slightly conservative 6 = Conservative 7 = Extremely conservative

Figure 5.2: Format of a Codebook

certain levels. These levels are called nominal, ordinal, interval, and ratio.

Nominal: At the nominal level, numbers are used to name or classify variables that have no quantitative differences. Religion, for example, would be a nominal-level variable because there is no quantitative difference between one religion and another. But in quantitative research, all information must be converted into numbers. Race, sex, organizational membership, marital status, day of week, and precinct are examples of other variables that are analyzed and measured at the nominal level.

Ordinal: Ordinal measures can be rank ordered; there are quantitative differences between categories. One response is higher or lower than another. Attitudes, for instance, are usually measured at the ordinal level.

Suppose respondents are asked how they feel about the following statement: "To reduce the U.S. trade deficit, Congress should impose tariffs on all manufactured goods." The answer "strongly agree" could be assigned a value of 5, whereas the answer "strongly disagree" is assigned a 1. The other categories, "agree," "neither agree nor disagree," and "disagree" could be assigned the values, 4, 3, and 2, respectively. Although the response categories for an ordinal measure can be rank ordered, the distance between the categories is not necessarily equivalent. In other words, the distance between "strongly agree" and "agree" may not be the same as the distance between "strongly disagree" and "disagree." The upshot of this is that values cannot be subtracted from or added to each other for analytical purposes. In terms of intensity of agreement, two respondents—one who "strongly agrees" with an issue and one who "strongly disagrees"—are not equivalent to two other respondents, both of whom "neither agree nor disagree," even though in both cases the individual values add to 6.

The ordinal measures we have discussed so far are *partially ordered*; that is, some responses or elements may have the same value. Ordinal measures may also be *fully ordered*, which means that each case has a unique value and may be rank ordered from highest to lowest. For example, grade point averages are often used to rank order students in a graduating class.

Interval: With interval levels, the distance between the response categories is equal. Thus the values can be added or subtracted from each other. Take for example, IQ scores. The distance between 100 and 110 is the same as the distance between 120 and 130. However, because there is no true zero as a starting point, the differences cannot be multiplied or divided. Someone with an IQ of 200 is not twice as smart as one with a score of 100. Few concepts of interest to precision journalists have the properties of the interval level of measurement.

Ratio: Variables measured at the ratio level do have a true zero point, and therefore can be added, subtracted, divided, and multiplied. Age, years of formal education, and income are examples. A person who is 50 years old is twice as old as one who is 25. And the difference between a person 50 years old and one 25 is the same as the difference between one 40 years old and another who is 15.

Sometimes, to simplify the analysis, data is moved from one level of measurement to another by collapsing categories. For instance, age, a ratio measure, can be converted to an ordinal one by using ranges such as 18-25, 26-35, 36-45, 46-55, and 56 and older. In doing this, the categories take on new values—that is, 18-25 becomes 1; 26-35 becomes

2; 36-45 becomes 3, and so on. Although collapsing categories simplifies the analysis, be aware that information is lost in the process.

Statistics That Describe

Some of the most widely used univariate descriptive statistic are frequency, ratio, proportion, percentage, rates, and measures of central tendency.

Frequency: Frequency is the number of times something occurs. If a sample contains 1,000 respondents and half of them are male, the frequency of male respondents is 500.

Ratio: Ratios are used to compare one group to another. A ratio is the quantity of one group divided by the quantity of the other. For example, if there are 150 people under 35 and 75 people over 35, the ratio of the first group to the second is 150/75—2 to 1, or 2:1. That is, there are two people under 35 for every one person over 35.

Proportion: A proportion is the ratio of one group to the total. For example, the proportion of people in the example here who are under 35 is obtained by dividing the number of those under 35 by the total: 150 divided by 225 equals .667.

Percentage: A percentage, sometimes called a *relative frequency*, is simply a proportion multiplied by 100. In the preceding example, for example, 66.7% of the total sample is under 35. To find a percentage change, divide the difference between the new and the original frequency by the original frequency. The formula is as follows:

$$\frac{\text{New Frequency} - \text{Original Frequency}}{\text{Original Frequency}} = \text{Percentage Change}$$

For example, suppose the number of voters in a community increased from 20,000 to 24,000. The original frequency is 20,000 and the new frequency is 24,000. Plugging in the appropriate numbers:

$$\frac{24{,}000 - 20{,}000}{20{,}000} = \frac{4{,}000}{20{,}000} = .20$$

Thus the number of voters increased by 20%. Now suppose the number of voters in a neighboring community dropped from 24,000 to 20,000. In this case we get:

$$\frac{20{,}000 - 24{,}000}{24{,}000} = \frac{-4{,}000}{24{,}000} = -.167$$

The number of voters in the second community decreased by 16.7%.

Rates: A rate is obtained when a frequency, such as the number of crimes, is divided by the total population and then multiplied by a constant to bring it to a whole number instead of a fraction or a proportion. A rate involves a period of time during which the events can accumulate. If, for example, a major U.S. city had 5,000 violent crimes in 1985 and its population was 1 million, the rate per capita would be 5,000 divided by 1,000,000, or .005 for the one-year period. But because the proportion is cumbersome, it is multiplied by a constant to make it a whole number. Crime rates are usually expressed in number of crimes per 100,000 residents, so the proportion is multiplied by 100,000. Thus for the year the crime rate would be 500 crimes per 100,000 residents. Rates are ratio measures.

Measures of central tendency: Except for rates, the statistics just discussed can be used with any level of measurement. Measures of central tendency—the mean, the median, and the mode—on the other hand, are used only with interval or ratio data.

The *mean* is what is most often thought of as the "average." It is the sum of the individual values divided by the number of cases. The mean, or average, age of three people age 40, 30, and 20 is 30 because $(40 + 30 + 20)/3 = 30$. Although the mean is widely used as a measure of the "average," it can be very sensitive to extreme values. Say, for instance, the average income of four brothers is $23,250, but one makes $12,000, two make $13,000, and the fourth makes $55,000. The $23,250 is arrived at of course by adding the four incomes and dividing by four. When working with data that have extreme values, it is often better to find the average by using the median.

The *median* is the midpoint value, derived by arraying the values and finding the one that lies in the middle, or in the case of an even number of values, the average of the two in the middle. The median income of the four brothers then is $13,000. The average value of a home in the United States, for example, is typically reported as a median value because a small percentage of very expensive homes place the mean value of a home much higher than the typical American owns.

The *mode* is simply the value that occurs most frequently in a distribution. If two or more values are "tied" with the most cases, the mode takes on the lowest value. The mode is seldom used.

ANALYZING THE DATA

To analyze data for one variable, you first compare the differences between the values of the categories for that variable. Suppose, for instance, randomly sampled respondents were asked the question, "What do you think is the most serious community problem?" and 10% of them said lack of downtown parking, 36% said high taxes, 34% said poor water quality, and 20% said crime. Before you can conclude, however, that high taxes is the problem citizens think is the most serious, you have to consider whether the differences in the values are a function of sampling error. Statistics for assessing sampling error are discussed in Chapter 8.

NOTES

1. The story appeared in the *Miami Herald*, February 15, 1982.

6

THINKING ABOUT THE WORLD

Explanatory research involves studying relationships between concepts.

On April 16, 1985, the North Carolina House voted 62-51 against toughening its antipollution laws. The outcome pleased businesses that faced potentially higher pollution control costs; it angered environmentalists. And it attracted the attention of the *Charlotte Observer*.[1]

At the time, reporters for the *Observer* were investigating the relationship between campaign contributions and voting patterns of legislators. The pollution issue presented an opportunity to test their hypothesis.

Their findings: Lawmakers who received campaign contributions from businesses opposed to the pollution measure were much more likely to vote against it than those who received no contributions, 66% versus 33%.

HYPOTHESES

A *hypothesis* is an untested statement intended to explain the relationship between two or more variables. The reporters' hypothesis probably was a statement such as this: Legislators who receive campaign contributions from businesses are less likely than those receiving no contribution to favor tougher antipollution laws. It contains three elements: an independent variable, a dependent variable, and a statement about the relationship between the two.

The *independent variable* is the cause; it does not depend upon something else for it to occur. The *dependent variable* is the effect; it does depend upon something else. When a variable is dependent in whole or in part on some other variable, the two variables are *related* or *associated*. Visually, an association or relationship between two variables is represented by an arrow:

INDEPENDENT VARIABLE ———> DEPENDENT VARIABLE
(Cause)   (Effect)

In the North Carolina antipollution law example, the independent variable is the campaign contribution; the vote on the antipollution is the dependent variable. The relationship between the two can be expressed by a statement that indicates how the values for the independent variable— received a contribution or did not receive a contribution— differs in terms of the dependent variable: Legislators who receive a contribution *will be more likely than* those who do not to oppose the antipollution measure.

It is a good idea to put hypotheses in writing before analyzing data. This makes it easier to discover and correct problems before it is too late. It is also helpful to state the independent variable first—the higher the education, the higher the income; the greater the exposure to reports of crime, the higher the level of fear of crime; the older one gets, the fewer movies one sees.

THE NATURE OF RELATIONSHIPS

To understand more clearly the nature of relationships, researchers must consider both the *direction* and *magnitude*, or intensity, of relationships. When the categories of the independent and dependent variables can be rank ordered, the direction of the relationship will be either positive or negative. Consider the three hypotheses mentioned earlier:

—The higher the education, the higher the income.
—The greater the exposure to news reports about crime, the greater the level of fear.
—The older one gets, the fewer movies one sees.

The first two are positive and the last one negative. Education is positively related to income, since as education increases so does income. Note that the same result could be achieved by reversing the hypothesis—the lower the education, the lower the income. The key to assessing whether two variables are positively related is to determine whether they change together in the same direction. In a negative relationship, as one variable goes up, the other variable goes down— they change in opposite directions. Thus as age increases, movie attendance decreases.

Positive and negative relationships can be visually portrayed in a scatterplot or scattergram (see Figure 6.1). The horizontal and vertical axes of the scatterplot represent the values of the independent and dependent variables, respectively. Each of the respondents or cases in a study can be plotted by finding the point that corresponds to their values on the independent and dependent variable scales. The spot in the scatterplot represented by the letter A in Figure 6.1 shows a person with 16 years of formal education who earns $25,000 a year. When all of the cases in a particular study are plotted in a scatterplot, a line is constructed that represents the best fit for all of the values. A positive relationship is evident when the best fitting line slopes upward; a negative relationship slopes downward. If there is no relationship between two variables, the line is horizontal.

When the independent variable is measured at the nominal level, the direction of a relationship is assessed by examining which value of the independent variable is more likely to exhibit a particular characteristic or value on the dependent variable. Returning to the introductory example, lawmakers who received contributions were hypothesized as being more likely than those who did not to oppose the antipollution measure. Similarly, if race affects voting preference, blacks would be more likely than whites to favor Candidate A and whites more likely to vote for Candidate B. When the dependent variable is nominal and the independent variable can be rank ordered, the relationship is also expressed as a likelihood. Thus the older people are when they get married, the less likely they are to get divorced.

The direction of a relationship, however, does not show how strongly two variables are related. Although direction is usually hypothesized before the data is analyzed, the magnitude of that relationship usually is assessed afterward. Because magnitude is a matter of degree, the adverbs "strongly," "moderately," and "weakly" are frequently used to describe a relationship.

Let us return to the *Observer* example. Remember, the reporters found that 66% of the lawmakers who received contributions and 33% of those who did not opposed the antipollution measure. Thus, as a group, lawmakers who received contributions were 33 percentage points more likely to oppose the measure than those who did not: 66% – 33%. But suppose the difference had been 55% and 45%. In this case, those who received contributions were only 10 percentage points more likely to be opposed. From this we see that as the percentage difference between two categories of an independent variable comes closer to 50%-50%, the weaker the relationship and, conversely, the more it tends toward the extreme, 100%-0%, the stronger the relationship.

We should also point out that a comparison between two studies is helpful but not necessary to assess the strength of a relationship. In the *Observer* study, the reporters found that lawmakers who received a

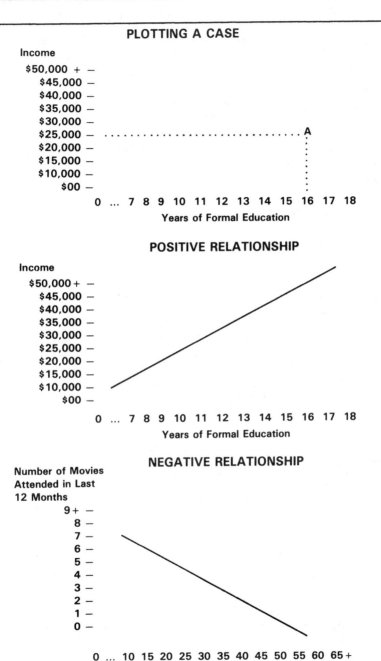

Figure 6.1: Scatterplots of Positive and Negative Relationships

contribution were twice as likely to oppose the antipollution measure, suggesting that the relationship between contributions and voting behavior is quite strong. Nevertheless, assessing the strength of a relationship can be difficult at times. To reduce the uncertainty, researchers frequently use other statistics. We address some of them in Chapters 7 and 8.

When no relationship or association exists between two variables, a *state of independence* exists. With two categories for both the independent and dependent variable, a complete state of independence is 50%-50%. Of course, one would not quibble about 51% versus 49% or 52% versus 48%; all suggest there is no relationship between the two variables. When two variables are completely related to each other—100% for one group versus 0% for the other—a *perfect* relationship exists. As you might expect, there are very few perfect relationships.

RESEARCH AND NULL HYPOTHESES

Two general categories of hypotheses are called the research hypothesis—the one we have been talking about—and the null hypothesis. The *research hypothesis,* sometimes called the alternative hypothesis, reflects your expectation of the relationship between two or more variables. Usually this means you believe one of the variables causes the other.

The *null hypothesis* is a statement that two variables are unrelated, that a state of independence exists. When analyzing relationships, a null hypothesis is tested rather than the research hypothesis because a relationship between two variables cannot be proved.

For example, you might hypothesize that the more time students study, the better they will do on an exam. The null hypothesis would be that studying has no effect on exam performance. If you found a relationship between studying and exam performance, you reject the null hypothesis and infer that studying was the cause. However, you have not proved studying improved exam performance. It could be that only the brightest students studied and intelligence, rather than studying, was the real cause. Because the number of independent variables that can account for a particular effect is limitless, relationships cannot be proved—only inferred.

Therefore, the two possible outcomes of testing the null hypothesis is to *reject* it and infer that the independent variable has an effect on the dependent variable or to *fail to reject* when you find no relationship between the variables.

Strictly speaking, researchers do not accept or reject research hypotheses, again because relationships cannot be proved. When rejecting the null hypothesis, they conclude that support has been found for the research hypothesis, an inference that holds until discredited or challenged by further research. Thus it is appropriate to say, "Legislators who received campaign contributions from businesses opposed to the antipollution measure were more likely to vote against the measure than those who did not," but not appropriate to conclude that campaign contributions actually caused the negative votes.

There are two final issues. The null and the research hypotheses can be identical. You may not believe a relationship exists yet you test it anyway just to be sure. Second, two different classes of statistics are used to test a null hypothesis—descriptive ones, such as the percentage and correlation coefficient, and inferential statistics. The first is always used and the second is used with probability samples, as we shall soon see.

THREE REQUIREMENTS OF CAUSE AND EFFECT

To establish cause and effect, three criteria must be satisfied:

(1) The cause must precede the effect.
(2) The cause and the effect must be associated or related.
(3) Other causes cannot be producing the effect of the cause under consideration.

The first of these three is usually the least difficult to ascertain. The campaign contributions were given at least a year before the legislators voted on the antipollution bill. Political values and party affiliations are usually formed before people vote.

Sometimes, though, establishing causal order is not so simple. Attitudes and beliefs do not always precede behavior. In fact, the opposite is frequently true. An interesting finding in consumer research is that attitudes toward a product frequently improve significantly after a person buys it. The purchase appears to "erase" negative feelings since they conflict with the actual behavior. To get around problems involved in causal ordering of attitudes and behaviors, researchers often conduct two or more studies, with at least one coming before the behavior, and the other, after.

The second criterion requires that a cause and effect be related. When there is a change in the independent variable, there must be a corresponding change in the dependent variable. Thus as education increases, income must also increase, otherwise there is no cause and effect relationship. This requirement of *covariation*, as it is sometimes called, is assessed through various statistical procedures, such as percentages and correlation coefficients.

The third criterion is the toughest and is in fact impossible to achieve, as we discussed earlier. You must demonstrate that no other variables are responsible for the effect produced by the independent variable. For example, suppose the hypothesis about the North Carolina legislative issue was that businesses opposing antipollution controls gave money only to legislators whom they believed supported their position.

Thus instead of the causal statement that says

CAMPAIGN CONTRIBUTION → VOTE ON ANTIPOLUTION MEASURE

we have a statement that says this is what really happened:

LEGISLATORS' OPINION   CAMPAIGN
BEFORE CAMPAIGN   ⟶   CONTRIBUTION
CONTRIBUTION
        ⟱
VOTE ON ANTIPOLLUTION MEASURE

In other words, the campaign contributions had no effect on the outcome of the vote. The results would have been the same whether or not there had been contributions. The *Observer* reporters could have obtained a measure of the legislators' opinions on pollution before the campaign to rule out this alternative hypothesis, but given the weight of the other evidence and the fact that they did not directly charge the businesses with bribery, it was not necessary. The foregoing again explains why the null hypothesis rather than the research hypothesis is tested. Because researchers can never prove that two variables are related, they can never completely rule out the infinite number of *confounding* variables that could account for the observed relationship. Though this is the case, precision journalists and social scientists are not doomed to stamp every finding "inconclusive." Replication of findings, logic, and mutual agreement among researchers are the foundations of sound research.

REMOTE VERSUS PROXIMATE CAUSES

Another important issue in cause and effect analysis is the distinction between *remote* and *proximate* causes. Consider the following:

CAMPAIGN CONTRIBUTION → FEELING OF INDEBTEDNESS→
VOTE IN FAVOR OF CONTRIBUTOR'S POSITION

Here a campaign contribution has an indirect effect on a lawmaker's voting behavior and would be considered a more remote cause. Generally the goal in research is to identify the most proximate cause—the variable or variables that have the most immediate effect. Thus the most proximate cause of opposing the antipollution measure may be the feeling of indebtedness associated with a campaign contribution. It is not always necessary or possible to measure the most proximate causes of behavior; indeed, the debate as to what constitutes a proximate cause can go on forever. But we bring this to your attention to emphasize that a reporter should be extremely leery of making causal statements.

SERENDIPITOUS FINDINGS

You will significantly reduce your chances of making incorrect observations if you hypothesize before rather than after the data have been collected and analyzed. An idea generated in advance can be disproved; one discovered later, by happenstance, cannot. You might accidentally find a relationship between two variables and you could not disprove it because the data already form a pattern. You then find yourself searching for an explanation to account for that relationship. This form of hypothesizing is called *ex post facto*, meaning it comes after the fact.

The danger of ex post facto hypothesizing is that logic will be sacrificed along the way. One of the things you will quickly learn as a researcher is that many behaviors and attitudes are related to or correlated with each other, but one does not necessarily cause the other. For instance, in northern states crime increases as ice cream consumption increases. Does one infer, then, that ice cream consumption causes crime or that crime causes ice cream consumption? Of course not. Crime increases during the summer because criminals, like the rest of us, stay indoors on cold winter nights.

Although the traditional method in research is to generate hypotheses before conducting the research, you need not dismiss unexpected but seemingly fortuitous findings. No one can logically anticipate all relationships. But you should scrutinize unexpected relationships, searching for confounding variables before accepting the *serendipitous* findings.

THEORY

Hypotheses are derived from theory. A *theory* is an idea about the way things are—an explanation for why something occurs or is.

An explanation must be empirically testable in order to be called a theory. Untestable explanations of the world—such as Creationism—technically cannot be called theories because they cannot be scrutinized with scientific methods. These types of explanations are referred to as philosophical doctrines.

Beyond the fact that a theory must be testable, researchers disagree as to what exactly constitutes one. Some argue that an explanation can only be labeled a theory if it is derived through deductive logic, a method social scientists have borrowed from the natural sciences. Others believe, and we agree, that any explanation for a relationship between two or more concepts that is testable can be called a theory. Thus a single hypothesis could encompass an entire theory, though this is rarely the case.

There are hundreds of theories about human behavior. Not all are valid and, as yet, none can provide a complete explanation of all behavior. Nevertheless, many theories have given us a better understanding of ourselves and the world around us.

Although theory is a prerequisite for explanatory research, it is seldom necessary for precision-journalism projects because reporters are generally interested primarily in issues that can be studied using descriptive analysis. Theory is not needed, for instance, to find out what percentage of the population supports abortion on demand. And precision journalists are not, as a rule, interested in solutions to complex social problems and behaviors; rather, they are interested in finding practical answers to everyday issues and problems. However, as precision journalism becomes more widespread, we believe there will be a greater attempt to explain the "why" as well as the "what."

ASSESSING OUTCOMES IN RESEARCH

The key to conducting good explanatory research is good ideas, or good theory. As simple as this principle seems, it is nonetheless often overlooked by beginning as well as seasoned researchers. It is easy to lose sight of original objectives and hypotheses when one finds a number of unexpected relationships. Remember, though, that even if a statistical association is found, it does not mean a cause and effect relationship exists. Furthermore, no statistical test can tell you whether a relationship exists—only your good sense can. Data should be used to test your ideas.

If good ideas initiate a project, you will not be disappointed. Support for your hypotheses is found and you take pride in what you have accomplished. Often, however, your hypotheses are not supported. What, then, do you do?

(1) Check to see if major errors were made when the data were entered into the computer or in the way they were analyzed.

(2) Rethink the original idea, theory, or hypothesis. It may have been incorrect. Everyone makes mistakes. That is part of the fun of research. Profit from them and, if necessary, modify or reject your original idea. On the other hand, do not be too quick to do so. If your idea seemed to make a great deal of sense to you and others around you, the problem may not be the idea, it may be the methodology you used or the way you operationalized your concepts.

(3) Check to see if the concepts were improperly operationalized. Do not underestimate the importance of this problem. One would expect, for example, that a person's income would be highly related to the price of an automobile he or she purchases. Although market researchers have found such a relationship, it is not as strong as you would expect. The reason is that income is usually measured by assessing total family income before taxes, which fails to take into account many other factors, such as the number of family members living on that income, the number of people contributing to that income, and the amount of debt. In short, disposable per capita family income would yield a much better relationship.

(4) Examine whether the appropriate research method was used. To test your ideas, you may have used a public opinion poll when content analysis of public records would have provided more accurate information.

NOTES

1. The series ran in the *Charlotte Observer*, June 16 to 20, 1985.

7

EXPLAINING THE WORLD

Percentage differences and correlation coefficients measure the strength of relationships between concepts.

Two weeks before the mayoral election, the city editor dumps a stack of computer printouts generated from the latest newspaper-sponsored election poll on your desk. "Look at these and give me a story that goes beyond the simple horse race. Why do voters prefer the candidate they do?" he says and walks away. You panic. "Where do I begin?" Before you look at those tabulations:

(1) Get some background information on the survey. Who conducted it? How was the population defined? How was the sample selected? What was the response rate?

(2) Get to know the issues and candidates. In this hypothetical election, the incumbent is Republican John Mason, a 48-year-old millionaire. As mayor, Mason trimmed the budgets of many city programs and successfully persuaded city council to pass an ordinance giving property tax breaks to business and industry. His challenger is Democrat Mary Williams, a 34-year-old social worker. The major thrust of her campaign is to improve social services for city residents, especially the indigent.

Now you are ready to generate some hypotheses to guide your analysis. To explain voter preference, you will look for differences between the candidates. When candidates disagree on a social issue or are of a different sex, race, age, or other physical or social category, you have an opportunity to explain why voters may prefer one candidate over the other. Of course, you would expect voters to favor candidates whose opinions and social characteristics are most like their own.

(3) Finally, write your ideas and hypotheses down. Because the incumbent is a male and the challenger a female, an obvious hypothesis is that male voters will favor the male candidate and female voters the female candidate.

Republican voters will prefer Mason, since he is the Republican candidate and Democratic voters will prefer Williams, the Democrat.

Since you know independent voters tend to vote for the more liberal candidate, you expect them to vote for Williams.

Since Mason is much wealthier than Williams, you assume high-income voters will be more likely to align themselves with Mason and lower-income voters with Williams.

During the campaign, Williams promised that as mayor she would improve social programs for single parents. Thus you expect single-parent voters to prefer her.

Now you are ready to turn to those tabulations.

CONTINGENCY TABLES

You begin by creating a *contingency* table from data you get from the computer printouts so that you can look at two variables simultaneously, a process called *bivariate analysis.*

Turn to your computer printouts and find the table that has the data listed for candidate preference by sex of voter. It should look something like Table 7.1, with a title, cells, cell frequencies and percentages, and marginal frequencies and percentages.

Title: The dependent variable is usually stated first in the title. It need not be as pithy as the one in Table 7.1, but it should be clear and concise.

Cells: Table 7.1 contains four cells, one for each possible combination when candidate preference is *crosstabulated* with sex of voter. The table has two rows and two columns and is called a 2 × 2 table. The rows correspond to the values of the dependent variable and the columns to those for the independent variable, the traditional way of constructing bivariate tables.

Cell frequencies and percentages: Each cell in the table contains two sets of numbers, the frequency or number of respondents in that cell and the percentage of the total in that column. For example, in the top left cell 400 of the 550 females, or 73%, say they intend to vote for the female candidate.

Marginal frequencies and percentages: At the far bottom right of the table is the total sample size. In this case N = 1,000. The numbers above the total and to the left are the *marginal* frequencies and percentages. These are the univariate descriptive statistics for the two variables. The table shows that 60% of the respondents intend to vote for Williams, the female candidate, and 40% for Mason, the male candidate. The marginals at the bottom show how many male and female voters there are: 550 females, 450 males. The marginal frequencies will add to N, the total number of respondents, and the marginal percentages to 100%, or thereabouts. The percentages may be off slightly because of rounding.

TABLE 7.1
Candidate Preference by Sex of Voter

	Sex of Voter		
	Female	Male	
Candidate Preferred			
Williams (Female)	400 73%	200 44%	600 60%
Mason (Male)	150 27%	250 56%	400 40%
	550 55%	450 45%	1,000 100%

Analyzing Percentage Differences

To see if the sex of the voter seems to influence candidate preference, look at the contingency table and compare the percentages. Table 7.1 shows that 44% of the males intend to vote for Williams compared to 73% of the females. Subtracting, you find that female voters are 29 percentage points more likely than males to prefer Williams, the female candidate. And males are 29 percentage points more likely than females to prefer Mason, the male candidate. These differences suggest, of course, that a voter's sex is related to or influences candidate preference.

A simple contingency table conveys a great deal of information. In this case you find the following:

- Williams leads Mason by a 20-percentage-point margin, 60% versus 40%;
- There are 10% more female voters than male voters, 55% versus 45%;
- Female voters are 29 percentage points more likely than male voters to prefer Williams and male voters are 29 percentage points more likely to prefer Mason;
- Female voters show a stronger preference for the female candidate than male voters do for the male candidate. Specifically, 73% of the female voters say they intend to vote for Williams but only 56% of the male voters intend to vote for Mason. Thus female voters are 17 percentage points more likely than males to prefer the candidate of their own sex.

As you can see, these findings are much more interesting than the simple horse race. In fact, this one table could become the basis for an entire story. The lead might be this: "Democratic challenger Mary Williams could easily defeat Mayor John Mason if the mayoral election were this week, according to a *Daily Star* telephone survey.

"The poll, conducted Oct. 21 to 24, gives Williams a 20-percentage-point lead over Mason. It also shows that male voters prefer Mason, whereas female voters prefer Williams. However, female voters seem to be more loyal to the candidate of their own sex. . . ."

Order of Variables in a Contingency Table

If the position of the dependent and independent variable is reversed, as in Table 7.2, the results will change because the base for generating the percentages becomes the categories of the candidate preference instead of sex. Table 7.2 shows that 66% of the respondents who prefer the female candidate are female, whereas 38% who prefer the male candidate are female. Although this is perhaps interesting, these findings do not speak to your hypothesis that voters' sex is related to candidate preference. We present these findings to illustrate how important it is to construct a contingency table with the independent variable on top.

BIVARIATE DESCRIPTIVE STATISTICS

Although precision journalists use percentages most of the time to analyze data, sometimes they need to use other descriptive statistics. This is particularly true when they are interested in comparing the relative strength of two different independent variables on the same dependent variable or when a contingency table has so many cells that comparing percentages would become a tedious task. Statistics that address these two issues are called measures of association or *bivariate descriptive statistics.*

The choice of statistic depends on how the variables are measured and sometimes on the number of categories you have. Most statistical software packages generate them for you automatically, although some are relatively easy to compute with a calculator. Some of the more widely used bivariate statistics for nominal and ordinal data are Yule's Q, Gamma, Lambda, Uncertainty Coefficient, Kendall's Tau b and Tau c, Phi, Cramer's V, Somer's d, and the Contingency Coefficient. Each has advantages and disadvantages and can be used only under certain conditions. You will want to consult other textbooks for more information on these statistics. But to see how they work, let us take a look at Yule's Q and Gamma.

Yule's Q

Yule's Q could be used to see, for example, how strong the relationship is between candidate preference and sex of the voter. Note

TABLE 7.2
Sex of Voter by Candidate Preference

	Candidate Preferred		
	Williams (Female)	Mason (Male)	
Voter Sex			
Female	400	150	550
	66%	38%	55%
Male	200	250	450
	33%	62%	45%
	600	400	1,000
	60%	40%	100%

that this statistic can be used only with a 2 × 2 table such as the one in Table 7.1, when the variables have only two categories and are measured at the nominal level. If you were working with ordinal, interval, or ratio data, you would have to use another statistic, or if appropriate, collapse your data into two categories. As mentioned in Chapter 5, collapsing categories has its problems, but subsequently we will discuss when it is appropriate to do so.

Computing Yule's Q is quite simple. If A is the top left cell in a 2 × 2 table, B the top right, C the bottom left, and D the bottom right, the formula is this:

$$\frac{AD - BC}{AD + BC} = \text{Yule's Q Value}$$

To see how this works, plug in the numbers from Table 7.1.

$$\frac{(400)(250) - (150)(200)}{(400)(250) + (150)(200)} = \frac{100,000 - 30,000}{100,000 + 30,000} = \frac{70,000}{130,000} = .54$$

The interpretation of Yule's Q can vary from situation to situation, but as a rule we suggest these guidelines:

.00 – .09	No relationship
.10 – .29	Weak relationship
.30 – .49	Weak to moderate relationship
.50 – .69	Moderate to strong relationship
.70 – .89	Strong to very strong relationship
.90 – 1.00	Very strong relationship

Since the value of Yule's Q for Table 7.1 is .54, the relationship between voter sex and candidate preference could be considered moderately strong.

Note that the value of Yule's Q ranges from −1.00 to +1.00 with the midpoint, or zero, indicating no relationship between the variables; +1.00 a perfect positive relationship; and -1.00 a perfect negative relationship. But because nominal data cannot be rank ordered, their relationships are usually not thought of as being positive or negative. Therefore, when interpreting the value of Yule's Q for a 2 × 2 table such as Table 7.1, you can ignore the sign. In other words, a value of −.50 means the same as +.50.

Gamma

Gamma is used with measures that can be rank ordered or with dichotomous nominal variables. Suppose, for example, you want to look at the relationship between income and candidate preference as shown in table 7.3. Candidate preference is a nominal, dichotomous measure and income is a ratio-level measure, collapsed into three categories. By using Gamma, a useful statistic for tables larger than 2 × 2, you will come up with values whose meanings are similar to those for Yule's Q. Because there are more categories, Gamma is more difficult to compute than Yule's Q, so we suggest you let the computer do it for you.

The value for Gamma in this case is .65, which suggests there is a moderately strong relationship between income and candidate preference. Higher-income voters prefer Mason; lower-income voters, Williams.

MEASURES OF ASSOCIATION FOR INTERVAL AND RATIO DATA

A correlation coefficient such as the Pearson product-moment coefficient is the primary statistic used to test the relationship of variables measured at the interval and ratio levels. Suppose, for example, you want to see if there is any relationship between crime rate and fear of crime in the United States. Your hypothesis is that as the crime rate increases, fear of crime increases.

Look at the scatterplot shown in Figure 7.1. The horizontal axis represents the values of the independent variable, crime rate, and the vertical axis represents those for the independent variable, fear of crime. Each of the dots represents a city whose population is 100,000 or more.

TABLE 7.3
Candidate Preference by Income

	Income		
	Under $20,000	$20,000-$49,999	$50,000 or More	
Candidate Preferred				
Williams	240	350	10	600
	80%	58%	10%	60%
Mason	60	250	90	40%
	20%	42%	90%	
	300	600	100	1,000
	30%	60%	10%	100%

Gamma = .65

The values plotted along the vertical axis reflect the percentage of adults in each city afraid to walk alone at night in some areas near their home. The values on the horizontal axis represent the violent crime rate per 100,000 population for 1985.

The correlation coefficient measures the extent to which the cases deviate from an imaginary line that represents the best fit of the cases. When the cases are very close to the line, the correlation is very high; when they are widely dispersed, it is low. The data in Figure 7.1 is reproduced in Figure 7.2, example A, but this time it is shown with a line that minimizes the distances between the dots.

Using a computer to generate the correlation coefficient, you would find that the the correlation between crime rate and fear of crime is .67, considered high and positive. The value of the correlation coefficient ranges from –1.00 to +1.00, with 0.00 meaning no relationship.

However, had the cases been widely dispersed, as in example B in Figure 7.2, the correlation would have been zero, indicated by a horizontal line. The final scattergram in Figure 7.2, example C, shows a negative relationship, which means fear of crime declines as crime rates increase.

USING BIVARIATE STATISTICS
TO RECOMPUTE PERCENTAGES

We have made several references throughout this book to the fact that you should be cautious about collapsing categories for variables

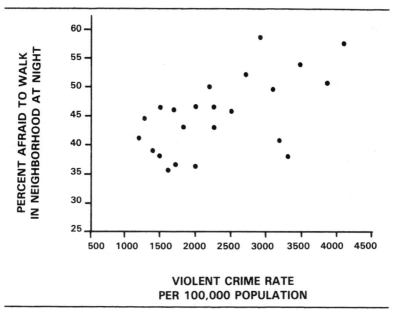

Figure 7.1: Fear of Crime by Violent Crime Rate

because information is lost when you do this. And, more important, relationships between variables can become distorted. In their natural or "raw" state, variables may be unrelated, but when categories are collapsed, sometimes a relationship seems to exist.

Values for any type of variable—whether nominal, ordinal, interval, or ratio—should not be collapsed to create relationships where none exists in their raw state. However, correlation coefficients and other bivariate statistics should not be used in news stories. The way around this problem is first to use bivariate statistics on the raw data, and if a relationship is found, collapse so that percentages can be presented in the news story.

Sometimes collapsing categories is no problem at all. For example, if your hypothesis is that white-collar workers will be more likely than blue-collar workers to prefer the Republican candidate, then occupations may be collapsed into two categories representing each of these two values. There is no need to examine the data in its raw state.

COMPARING RELATIONSHIPS

The interpretation of bivariate descriptive statistics is clearer if you evaluate them in a relative rather than an absolute context. For

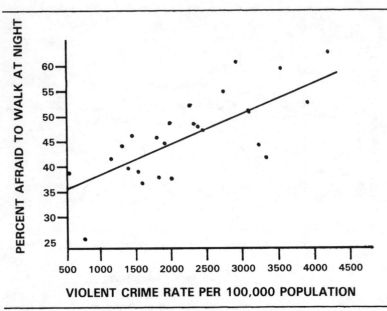

Figure 7.2A: Best Fitting Line for the Relationship Between Fear of Crime and Violent Crime Rate: Example A, Positive Relationship

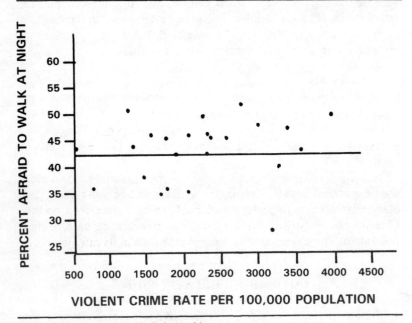

Figure 7.2B: Example B, No Relationship

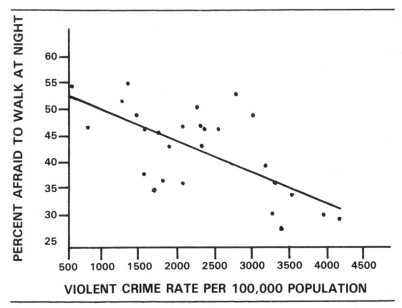

Figure 7.2C: Example C, Negative Relationship

example, you might want to determine whether sex or parental status has a stronger effect on candidate preference.

Recall that parental status was selected as an independent variable because Williams, the Democrat, had pledged to create new city services designed to meet the needs of single-parent families. Parental status then is coded as a dichotomy, with single-parent voters in one category and all other voters in the other. Table 7.4 shows the relationship between candidate preference and parental status.

Note first that single-parent voters are 33 percentage points more likely than all other voters to prefer the female candidate. This is slightly higher than the 29 percentage point difference found for sex, and this difference is confirmed by Yule's Q, which has a value of .67 compared to .54 for sex. Since Gamma is the equivalent of Yule's Q for ordinal data, you could conclude that income, with its Gamma value of .65, has just as strong an effect on candidate preference as parental status. Also note that although percentage differences for two different relationships may be equivalent, their respective bivariate measures of association may not be.

When comparing bivariate descriptive statistics be sure that the statistics are compatible. One statistic can always be compared with another of its kind, but usually different statistics cannot be compared

TABLE 7.4
Candidate Preference by Parental Status

| | Parental Status | | |
	Single Parent	All Others	
Candidate Preferred			
Williams	250	350	600
	83%	50%	60%
Mason	50	350	400
	17%	50%	40%
	300	700	1,000
	30%	70%	100%

Yule's Q = .67

to each other. Since Gamma cannot be computed for political party affiliation because that variable has three values and Yule's Q can only be used with dichotomous variables, you will have to rely upon percentages, find some other statistic that can be used with all of the different data, or recode the independent variable by collapsing categories so that Yule's Q can be computed.

MULTIVARIATE ANALYSIS

So far we have dealt with only one independent variable at a time. We saw how sex, income, and parental status—each taken separately—influence candidate preference. Although bivariate analysis yields valuable insights, it is not the final step in explanatory analysis.

Recall from Chapter 6 that three criteria are required for cause and effect: (a) a cause must precede an effect, (b) the cause and effect must be statistically related, and (c) other possible causes must be ruled out. Bivariate analysis meets the first two criteria quite well, but in order to assess the third, more than one independent variable must be examined at the same time. The goal of this third requirement is to rule out spurious effects.

To do this, researchers employ *multivariate* analysis, which requires advanced statistical procedures and unless you use them, you usually cannot draw conclusive cause and effect statements from nonexperimental research. It is quite acceptable to report that nonwhites are more likely than whites to favor welfare programs, but not that race causes attitudes toward welfare. As discussed in Chapter 6, you must examine other confounding or intervening variables, such as income and political party affiliation, to rule out spurious effects.

ARE THE DIFFERENCES SIGNIFICANT?

Throughout this chapter we have examined how explanatory hypotheses are tested with bivariate and multivariate statistics. We have emphasized differences to illustrate various statistical techniques. But how much of a difference is significant? Where does a researcher draw the line in terms of assessing how important a difference is?

If the data come from an entire population, you rely completely upon descriptive statistics. The difference found in a population is a real difference. However, be sure the difference is large enough to be meaningful. When you have doubts, express them with a statement such as "The relationship between x and y is weak." Remember that when the data are drawn from a probability sample, you must use the inferential statistics discussed in the next chapter to determine whether your findings are a function of sampling error or whether they are likely to represent real differences in the population.

8

MAKING INFERENCES TO POPULATIONS

**Inferential statistics estimate population characteristics
and show whether differences are a function of sampling
error.**

Suppose you are assigned to write the story reporting the results of your
newspaper's pre-election telephone poll. The Republican candidate is
preferred by 53% of the respondents and the Democrat by 47%. The 600
respondents were randomly selected from the registered voters in your
community. Is the Republican candidate leading? If your answer is
"yes," you might want to review Chapter 4. As we noted then, all
probability samples contain sampling error and, in some cases, this
error can be responsible for differences observed in the data.

The purpose of this chapter is to show how *inferential statistics* can be
used to draw conclusions about a population from a limited number of
observations of that population. These statistics are used in two ways.
One is to estimate characteristics of populations from a probability
sample. Two is to determine whether differences observed in sample
data reflect real differences in the population or whether they could have
occurred by chance because of sampling error. Statistics for this second
purpose are called *tests of statistical significance*.

First we will discuss how population parameters are estimated. Keep
in mind that all of the statistical formulas presented in this chapter
assume simple random-sampling techniques were used to collect the
data.

ESTIMATING POPULATION PARAMETERS

Estimating population parameters involves a tradeoff between two
criteria—precision and accuracy. *Precision* refers to the exactness of an
estimate and *accuracy* to its correctness. And in a sample, the greater the
precision, the less the accuracy; and conversely, the greater the accuracy,
the less the precision. To see why, suppose you have before you a drum
filled with 10,000 balls. Half of them are white, the other half black.

With your eyes closed, you draw a sample of 100 balls from the drum—48 white ones and 52 black ones. Now, it would be very precise to say that 48% of the balls are white, but it would not be entirely accurate. Your estimate is off by 2%.

To correct for this, you can create a range around your sample finding so that with a great deal of confidence you can say that the percentage of white balls in the population is somewhere between 38% and 58%, plus and minus 10% of your sample finding. Although the accuracy of your estimate is greatly improved, it is not very precise because now you have a 20-percentage-point spread.

Estimating sampling error involves balancing precision and accuracy. *Standard error* is the technical term used to refer to the statistic that takes these two criteria into account.

Calculating Sampling Error for a Percentage

To estimate sample error, let us return to the telephone poll results. Recall that 53% of the voters preferred the Republican candidate and 47% the Democratic candidate. To compute the standard error, take the square root of the proportion of one response category multiplied by the proportion of the other and divided by the total sample size. The formula looks like this:

$$\text{Standard Error} = \sqrt{\frac{\text{Proportion Preferring Republican Candidate} \times \text{Proportion Preferring Democratic Candidate}}{\text{Total Sample Size}}}$$

Plugging in the numbers, the standard error in the election poll is 0.02, or 2%.

$$\text{Standard Error} = \sqrt{\frac{.53 \times .47}{600}} = .02$$

This percentage corresponds to the precision component. It is the range, either plus or minus the sample finding, within which you expect the true population parameter to lie. To estimate for accuracy, a confidence level must be selected.

Selecting a Confidence Level

Probability theory states that there is a 68% chance a true population parameter lies within the range of one standard error. For the telephone poll example, then, there is a 68% chance that 51% to 55% of the voters prefer the Republican candidate and that 45% to 49% prefer the Democrat. This level of confidence produces a high level of precision, but not a very high level of accuracy. There is a 32% chance that the true population parameter lies somewhere outside of the plus or minus 2-percentage-point *confidence interval* or range. In other words, you would be incorrect 32% of the time when estimating the population parameter.

Under most circumstances, you will want to be more accurate than that and, to do so, you must sacrifice some precision for more accuracy. Although there is no universal standard for determining how much precision should be traded for accuracy, the most widely used level of confidence is 95%. Researchers sometimes use 99% or 90%, but rarely do they use less than 90%.

To calculate sampling error for a 95% level of confidence, simply multiply the standard error by 1.96. In the elections example, the confidence interval now goes from 2% to 4%. Hence there is a 95% chance that in the population of voters 49% to 57% prefer the Republican candidate and 43% to 51% prefer the Democratic candidate. To calculate sampling error for a 90% level of confidence, multiply the standard error by 1.65; for 99%, multiply by 2.58.

Finally, in order to compute sampling error for a variable that has more than two response categories, select one category and lump all of the others into a second category. If a variable has a large number of response categories, such as age or income, you calculate the standard error for the mean. A statistical software package will do this for you.

Comparing Differences with Sampling Error

In addition to estimating population parameters, the standard error can show whether the difference between the Republican and Democratic candidates could have occurred by chance because of sampling error. Using a 95% level of confidence, what would you conclude about the election race? In a nutshell, it is too close to call. The confidence intervals for each of the candidates overlap; that is, 51% of the voters could prefer the Democratic candidate and 49% the Republican candidate. You cannot say with 95% confidence that the Republican candidate leads the Democratic candidate. The chances are actually greater than 5%, the converse of 95%, that the observed difference is due to sampling error.

Additional Comments About Sampling Error

As noted in Chapter 4, sampling error is heavily influenced by the size of the sample. The larger the sample, the smaller the error. For example, if 1,000 instead of 600 voters had been interviewed, the difference between the Republican and Democratic candidates would have been *statistically significant*, meaning you could conclude with 95% confidence that the Republican candidate is, indeed, leading in the election.

Before leaving this discussion of sampling error, we must again draw attention to the fact that the standard error formula is based on data drawn from random-sampling procedures. If the cases represent the entire population, there is no need to calculate the sampling error because the sample findings are identical to the population parameters, and if nonprobability sampling techniques are used, sampling error cannot be calculated.

Two other assumptions are usually made when calculating the sampling error—a 100% response rate and no nonsampling measurement errors. Of course, neither is likely to be achieved in most survey research situations. As a rule, though, the more they are violated the less reliable the sample findings. Unfortunately, it is usually difficult if not impossible to measure the extent to which they are violated. But even if they are not violated, you must keep in mind that there is still a 5% chance with a 95% level of confidence that the sample result will fall outside of the confidence interval. In short, be cautious before you stake your reputation on one statistic. Keep sampling error in perspective: Like all statistics, it is a tool for reducing the amount of subjectivity involved in decision making—it should not replace the decision itself.

TESTS OF SIGNIFICANCE FOR ONE VARIABLE

Sampling error is one way to determine whether a significant difference exists between two categories of one variable only. Another is the *Z Test for mutually exclusive categories.*

Z Test for Mutually Exclusive Categories

The Z Test also shows if the difference between two categories of one variable is significantly different. The test yields a value, appropriately called the *Z value*, which, when equal to or greater than 1.65, means a difference is statistically significant at the 90% level of confidence and not likely to be a function of sampling error. If the Z value is equal to or greater than 1.96, then the difference is statistically significant at the 95% level of confidence, and values equal to or greater than 2.58 are significant at the 99% level.

For this test, the categories of a variable must be mutually exclusive, but there is no limit to the number of categories. And the percentages being compared do not have to add up to 100% as they do when calculating standard error.

Suppose a random sample of voters were asked to chose their favorite among four candidates running in an election. The computer printout shows that 40% prefer Candidate 1, 30% prefer Candidate 2, 25% prefer Candidate 3, and 5% prefer Candidate 4. Clearly, three of the candidates are leading Candidate 4—you do not need a statistical test to see that. But is Candidate 1 leading Candidate 2 and is Candidate 2 leading Candidate 3, or could these differences simply be a function of sampling error?

To run the Z Test, use the following equation. P1 and P2 represent the proportion of respondents preferring Candidate 1 and Candidate 2, respectively.

$$Z = \frac{P1 - P2}{\sqrt{\dfrac{(P1)(1 - P1) + (P2)(1 - P2) + 2(P1)(P2)}{N}}}$$

Plugging in the appropriate numbers:

$$Z = \frac{.40 - .30}{\sqrt{\dfrac{(.40)(.60) + (.30)(.70) + 2(.40)(.30)}{600}}} = 2.94$$

Since the value of Z, 2.94, is greater than 2.58, you can say with 99% confidence that Candidate 1 is leading Candidate 2. In other words, the probability is less than 1% that the observed difference is due to sampling error. Of course, this also means that Candidate 1 leads Candidates 3 and 4 as well, since the proportions for these later candidates are less than that for Candidate 2. Computing Z for the difference between Candidates 2 and 3 yields a value of 1.66—significant at the 90% level of confidence, but not at 95%. Since most of the time a 95% level of confidence is used, you could not say with confidence that Candidate 2 leads Candidate 3. You would conclude that it is not clear which candidate is running second.

Z Test for Overlapping Groups

If you are interested in determining whether there is a significant difference between two categories of a measure that allows respondents to give more than one answer—a *multiple-response* measure—then you would use the *Z Test for overlapping groups*. Suppose respondents are asked to name what they believe to be the major problems facing the economy. Assume 40% say the deficit is the major problem, 30% say the trade imbalance, and 10% say both the deficit and trade. With a sample size of 600 is the difference between 40% and 30% statistically significant? The formula is as follows:

$$Z = \frac{P1 - P2}{\sqrt{\dfrac{[(P1)(1-P1) + (P2)(1-P2) + 2(P2P2 - P12)]}{N}}}$$

P12 represents the proportion of those who cited both deficit and trade—in other words, the proportion of the overlap. Now we plug in the numbers:

$$Z = \frac{.40 - .30}{\sqrt{\dfrac{(.40)(.60) + (.30)(.70) + [(.40)(.30) - .10]}{600}}} = 3.50$$

The Z value, 3.50, is greater than 2.58; therefore, you can conclude with at least 99% confidence that in the population of voters the deficit is, indeed, considered to be a bigger problem than the trade imbalance.

TESTS OF STATISTICAL SIGNIFICANCE
FOR TWO VARIABLES

The principle behind tests of statistical significance for two variables is the same as that for one variable. Given a certain level of confidence they indicate whether a sample result is likely to be a function of sampling error.

Chi-Square

Chi-square is one of the most widely used tests of statistical significance for crosstabular data. Instead of a Z value, chi-square yields a value based on sampling distribution that shows how likely it is that something could have occurred by chance.

Suppose the results of a poll indicate that 59% of the 800 respondents surveyed support the Equal Rights Amendment; 41% oppose it. You wonder if a person's education is related to his or her attitude toward the amendment. If education were in no way related, you would expect that approximately 59% of respondents in each educational-level category would say they were in favor of the amendment; 41% would say they were opposed. However, Table 8.1, part A, shows that only 50 of 200, or 25%, of those with less than a high school education said they favored the ERA, whereas 300 of 350, or 86%, of those with a college degree said they did. Your *observed* percentages for these two categories then are 25% and 86%. Does this mean that educational level is related to support for the ERA or is the difference between the expected and observed values just happenstance—caused by sampling error?

In this case, after running a chi-square test, you could safely assume that there is a relationship. This is why.

The extent to which an expected frequency varies from the observed frequency is used to determine if a relationship could have occurred by chance. The closer the expected frequency is to the observed frequency, the more likely it is that the results are a function of sampling error. Conversely, the greater the disparity, the more likely the observed results reflect a real difference in the population.

To calculate the expected frequency for a cell, multiply the two marginal frequencies and divide by the total sample size. From Table 8.1, part B, plug in the numbers from cell A—the top left cell: Expected frequency = $(475 \times 200)/800 = 119$. Again, if there were no relationship between educational level and support for ERA, you would expect this cell to have a frequency of 142. As we can see, however from part A, the observed frequency for cell A is 50, a considerable difference.

After all the expected frequencies are calculated, as they are in Table 8.1, part B, the numbers are plugged into the chi-square formula:

$$\chi^2 = \Sigma \frac{(0 - E)^2}{E}$$

Sigma (Σ) means that the findings for each cell are summed. Computing chi-square for the data in Table 8.1 yields the following:

$$\chi^2 = \left[\frac{(50 - 119)^2}{119} + \frac{(125 - 148)^2}{148} + \frac{(300 - 208)^2}{208} + \right.$$

$$\left. \frac{(150 - 81)^2}{81} + \frac{(125 - 102)^2}{102} + \frac{(50 - 142)^2}{142} \right]$$

$$\chi^2 = 40.0 + 3.6 + 40.7 + 58.8 + 5.2 + 59.6$$

TABLE 8.1
Support for ERA by Educational Level

(A) Observed Frequencies and Percentages

	Education			
Support ERA	Less than High School	High School, Some College	College Degree	Total
Yes	50 (25%)	125 (50%)	300 (86%)	475
No	150 (75%)	125 (50%)	50 (14%)	325
	200	250	350	800

(B) Expected Frequencies and Percentages

	Education			
Support ERA	Less than High School	High School, Some College	College Degree	Total
Yes	119 (59%)	148 (59%)	208 (59%)	475
No	81 (41%)	102 (41%)	142 (41%)	325
	200	250	350	800

$$\chi^2 = 207.9$$

To determine whether this value, 207.9, is statistically significant, the *degrees of freedom* for the table must be calculated. The formula is:

$$df = (rows - 1) \times (columns - 1)$$

Because this example has two rows and three columns you find there are two degrees of freedom: $(2-1) \times (3-1) = 2$. Turn to the chi-square table in Appendix C and find the row corresponding to degrees of freedom and level of confidence you require—95% in most cases. If the value of chi-square is equal to or greater than the critical value shown in the chi-square table, then the observed relationship is not likely to be a function of sampling error.

In this case, the critical value needed for chi-square to be statistically significant is 5.99. Since 207.9 far exceeds this critical value, sampling error is not likely to account for the observed difference between levels of education.

A limitation to chi-square should be noted. If any expected frequency is less than 5, chi-square will not produce reliable results. A correction factor must be employed, some other statistical test will be necessary, or categories of either the independent or dependent variable must be collapsed to increase the number of expected frequencies.

Z Test for Two Independent Groups

Another useful *bivariate test of significance* is the Z Test for two independent groups. Independent here means that the two groups are mutually exclusive—a case cannot be in both groups at the same time. As with the other Z Tests, when the value of Z is equal to or exceeds 1.96, the difference is statistically significant at the 95% level of confidence.

Two steps are involved in calculating this test. First, P prime (P′) is calculated and then the value is inserted into another formula to compute Z. For example, suppose 35% of white voters and 50% of black voters favor busing. Assume 1,000 of the respondents in this random sample are white and 100 are black. Is the difference between the opinions of the whites and blacks statistically significant? The formula for calculating Z begins by calculating P prime:

$$P' = \frac{(N1)\,(P1) + (N2)\,(P2)}{N1 + N2}$$

Inserting the appropriate numbers:

$$P' = \frac{(1000)\,(.35) + (100)\,(.50)}{1000 + 100} = .40$$

After P′ is calculated, go on to the second step:

$$Z = \frac{P1 - P2}{\sqrt{\dfrac{(P')\,(1 - P') \times (N1 + N2)}{(N1)\,(N2)}}}$$

$$Z = \frac{.35 - .50}{\sqrt{\dfrac{(.40)\,(.60) \times (1000 + 100)}{(1000)\,(100)}}} = -2.92$$

Because Z is greater than 1.96, you can conclude with 95% confidence that, in the population of voters, blacks are more likely than whites to favor school busing.

STATISTICAL SIGNIFICANCE FOR LARGE SAMPLES

Because sampling error is primarily a function of sample size, relatively large samples—those greater than 1,500—will yield statistically significant findings for very small differences. Therefore, if the sample is large, the analysis should concentrate on *substantive* differences rather than statistically significant ones. To do this, use the descriptive statistics discussed in Chapters 5 and 7.

9

WRITING AND PRESENTING FINDINGS

Proper analysis of data is crucial in a precision-journalism project, but the findings won't be useful unless they are clearly written and presented.

[By Joseph R. Tybor and Mark Eissman
Staff writers, the *Chicago Tribune*.]

What began as a birthday party one Thursday night in June three years ago turned into an ordeal for Orlando Rivera, who spent the next 12 days in Cook County Jail because he could not afford bail.

Rivera, then 19 and a restaurant worker, was arrested for a crime he did not commit, but he served time in jail for it nonetheless. His case illustrates a serious inequity in the bail system in Chicago.

A computerized study of bail by the *Tribune* has concluded that more than 13,000 people spend time in jail each year for crimes the law is later unable to prove they committed. About 3,000 of them are incarcerated for more than two weeks, but in some rare cases for more than a year.

These people, although innocent in the eyes of the law, are punished more severely than the thousands of felons who stay free on bail before their trials and then are convicted and sentenced to probation.

Innocent people kept in jail each year for want of bail include an estimated 7,327 defendants without criminal records, the *Tribune* survey found. The survey closely examined 2,759 felony cases in Chicago during a 13-month period in 1983-84.

Before being taken into custody on June 3, 1982, Orlando Rivera had no criminal record. He had lived in Chicago since age 3, was sharing an apartment with his parents and was engaged to be married.

Over the next 12 days in jail, he contends, he was beaten twice by guards and lost his job. . . .

Thus began a story in a series about the Illinois bail system that appeared June 3, 1985. The following day, another story by Tybor and Eissman appeared, which detailed the other side of the problem. Some excerpts follow:

Late each afternoon, the phone would ring. Whenever the 17-year-old girl answered, there was heavy breathing on the line. For weeks she was terrified.

A junior at an all-girl Catholic high school on the Southwest Side, she was scheduled to testify against the man charged with trying to rape her.

The man charged in the crime, Rosario Infelice, had been apprehended within hours of the incident on Dec. 31, 1983, on the basis of information she provided police, including the license number of his car. The girl identified him at a police lineup.

At the time, Infelice was free on bond and awaiting trial in a rape case two months earlier. But when he appeared before a judge on the new charge, the bond was not revoked.

Instead, he was allowed to remain free after paying an additional $5,000. And when he was arrested a few days later in connection with another attempted rape, he paid $20,000 more and went back on the streets.

Eventually, Infelice was convicted of unlawful restraint for the attack on the teenage girl. Right after the trial, the menacing phone calls stopped.

But the fact that he could post bond three times for the same sort of violent offense has left his young victim extremely bitter. . . .

In Illinois, there has never been a definitive study of crime committed by people on bail. However, an extensive computer survey by the *Tribune* of the bail system in Chicago suggests that the problem may be a serious one here.

The study of 2,759 felony cases. . . . [1]

After presenting their analysis of the computer data, the *Tribune* reporters concluded that because the bail system in Chicago relied on money innocent people were locked up because they did not have as little as a $100 to pay for bail; but dangerous people, with access to large amounts of money, went free until they were sentenced to prison.

Three and a half months after the series ran, Illinois Governor James Thompson signed into law a bill that addressed the problems uncovered by this impressive precision-journalism project. It would not have had the impact it did if the stories had been presented merely as a series of statistics from the reporters' computer analysis.

Proper analysis of data is absolutely crucial to the success of a precision-journalism project. But no research project—no matter how well done—will inform and educate if the stories reporting the findings are poorly or blandly written. Writing a story from dozens of numerical facts and making it interesting is a challenge as great as any in journalism.

Let us take a look at some other examples of how reporters have tackled the problem of writing readable stories from the results of their precision-journalism projects, examine some of the ethical issues involved in research, and consider some ideas for projects based on the methods described in this book.

THE LEAD

For most writers, the lead is the most difficult part of a story to write. There are of course any number of ways to start a story, but basically leads fall into two categories: the direct or summary lead and the delayed or feature lead.

Direct Leads

Just as the term implies, the direct lead gets to the point—fast. The object is to summarize key findings in as few words as possible. Give the most important fact or facts, and then expand on them—the inverted pyramid in its classic form. Here are some examples:

> Proposals for a Missouri state lottery and horse-track betting continue to enjoy solid support from voters questioned in a recent (St. Louis) *Post-Dispatch*/KMOX radio opinion poll [October 2, 1984].

> Centerville is the toughest town in Michigan on drunk drivers, and Grosse Pointe Farms is the easiest, a *Detroit News* study shows [May 12, 1985].

> The trend toward more and more women working is good for the economy and for society as a whole, according to men and women responding to a *Milwaukee Sentinel survey* [April 22, 1985].

Simple and straightforward, the direct lead is most frequently used for timely news events, such as those that stem from voter and public opinion polls.

Delayed Lead

For older news, news that requires some background information, or for in-depth precision-journalism projects, reporters frequently turn to the delayed or feature lead. Investigative or in-depth precision-journalism projects, such as the *Chicago Tribune*'s investigation of the bail system, frequently use anecdotes. The idea is to select one or more cases that summarize either the purpose of the research or the key findings.

The cases do not have to come from the data collected, but they should reflect the essence of the findings, such as in the following extracts:

> The 32-year-old woman browsing through a rack of sexually-explicit videotapes at a downtown adult bookstore scoffed at the Maricopa County attorney's recent crackdown on obscenity.
>
> "Whether they are sold up front or under the table, people are going to get them or make them themselves," she said last week.
>
> At another bookstore, a 22-year-old Arizona State University student dressed in Bermuda shorts and a T-shirt agreed.
>
> "That's garbage," he said, referring to the announced assault on bookstore and video-store owners who offer allegedly obscene tapes and movies.
>
> The student and the woman said people should have the right to view such materials—particularly in their own homes.
>
> An overwhelming number of the 600 people surveyed in Maricopa and Pima counties two weeks ago in a scientific poll commissioned by the *Arizona Republic* agreed with the two [May 12, 1985].[2]

> Something had gone wrong at Memorial Hospital in South Bend, Ind. Nearly one of every four Medicare patients who entered Memorial in 1984 for coronary bypass surgery—27 of 119 people—died, some on the operating table, some in recovery, all before they could go home. It was the worst record in the nation that year, according to a computer analysis by the (Detroit) *Free Press* Washington bureau.
>
> "They still haunt me," said Dr. Ross Gardner, one of Memorial's two principal heart surgeons at the time. "It's horrible. You wake up nights and start thinking about what you did wrong."
>
> Eighty miles away, at Lutheran Hospital in Ft. Wayne, Ind., only one of 78 Medicare patients admitted for coronary bypass surgery died in 1984. The contrast between Memorial and Lutheran illustrates one fact about coronary bypasses, the most common major operation in America: Where a patient goes for the surgery can mean the difference between life and death [September 21, 1986].[3]

Instead of anecdotes, some reporters use analogies:

> It's easy to equate divorce with death, and consider marriage the corpse. Yet the severing of marital ties often resembles labor pains and the birth of

a new and better life for at least one of the former partners and in many cases, children from the marriage.

Far from being a totally negative experience, divorce can give people a second (in some cases a third or fourth) chance to find happiness alone or with another partner.

That is one conclusion that can be drawn from responses to the *Indianapolis Star*'s 189-question survey on Divorce in Marion County [February 26, 1985].

A third approach is to provide some perspective or background information before presenting the key finding:

Superintendents of the biggest school districts in the country are at odds with Dallas parents, students and teachers over one oft-discussed remedy for the ills of U.S. education.

The superintendents say American students, like their Japanese and European peers, should spend longer hours and more days in school, but both ideas were rejected by wide margins by parents, students and teachers polled by the *Dallas Times Herald* [December 11, 1983].[4]

A fourth approach might be called novel writing. The purpose is to set the stage or a mood before introducing the major findings.

The chimes echo through the state Legislative Building at 1:30 p.m., summoning to duty an auto dealer, a farmer, a retired teacher, an insurance salesman, a lawyer.

In the rotunda, a lobbyist trying to get in a last word, follows a senator to one of the 750-pound brass doors to the chamber. A secretary thrusts another pink telephone message at a harried House member whose business back home suffers in his absence.

Inside the chambers, gavels bang, prayers are said, and the N.C. House and Senate come alive for another session.

Since 1776, citizen-legislators have come to the capital, leaving behind jobs and families, gathering under one roof in a club of legislators, aides, and lobbyists to write the laws that govern North Carolina's citizenry.

For the 170 legislators meeting since February as the 1985 General Assembly, the cost of membership was $1.54 million. Some of the money for their campaigns came from citizens they represent back home.

But large sums also came from sources with big stakes in the 1985 session:

from the candidates and from statewide interests that contribute to political campaigns as deliberately as they lobby the winners who go to Raleigh.

An (Charlotte) *Observer* study of 267 House and Senate campaigns found a recurring connection between political contributions and legislative activity. The most active contributors last year were people or groups whose financial interests are the most heavily lobbied in the General Assembly.

The *Observer*'s five-month examination—the most extensive ever of campaign finance reports filed since 1974 by N.C. legislative candidates— raises questions about whose voices are heard loudest in Raleigh [June 16, 1985].[5]

A fifth approach uses the second person.

If you're typical, you'll see a doctor almost five times this year. If your doctor is typical, he won't have time to give you the care he'd like.

There are 252,000 of you swamping 177 of them in the nine-county Dubuque Health Service Area.

And swamped they are, they said in response to a (Dubuque) *Telegraph Herald* survey of physicians [August 17-24, 1975].

OTHER ELEMENTS OF PRECISION JOURNALISM STORIES

Of course, a lead is not the only element of a precision-journalism story. Reporters must support their major findings or conclusions with the specific facts and statistics they gathered during their research. An effective way to accomplish this is to present the data graphically, that is, with graphs and charts. Needless to say, rattling off a list of numbers and percentages can get monotonous rather quickly. Graphics, however, can effectively combat this problem and at the same time stimulate interest in a story.

A precision-journalism story must also include background information, such as the type of methodology used, special problems in data collection, and an estimate of sampling error.

Finally, note that the news-gathering process in a precision-journalism project is not limited to the statistics that pop out of a computer. Almost always it includes news gathered through traditional techniques— details from interviews with people involved with or affected by the project. Some of the best insights come from outside the data set.

Presenting Data Graphically

In a news story, data may be presented graphically or in tabular form. Except when it is necessary to convey vast amounts of information, a graphic presentation is better. A picture is much more interesting and, more important, summarizes and conveys the information more quickly than a table of numbers.

Nearly all forms of data can be presented in bar, line, or pie charts. A pie chart works well to display percentages that total 100%. As a rule, a pie chart should have no more than six "slices"; more makes it difficult to compare the size of the slices (see Figure 9.1).

Bar and line charts work well to display changes over time and are also appropriate for multiple responses from open-ended questions (see Figures 9.2. 9.3, and 9.4). Bar charts should nearly always begin at zero or the lowest value for the measure to avoid distorting data (see Figure 9.5).

Charts should include the title or the question asked and the numerical value, clearly identified as a frequency, percentage, mean, or median. Information about research procedures and sample size should be included in the accompanying story, but it can be included as part of the graphic. When graphically presenting the findings for two variables, bar and line charts are usually better than pie charts because comparing slices in two or more pies is sometimes difficult. A chart should be constructed so that comparisons are made between values of the independent variable. The values of the independent variable should be compared because the findings will be reported as follows: "High-income voters are more likely than low-income voters to be members of the Republican Party. The reverse is true for the Democratic Party" (see Figure 9.6).

When the dependent variable is dichotomous, it is not necessary to present the findings for both values. For example, if sex is the independent variable and opinion of the Equal Rights Amendment is the dependent, all that is needed is two bars, one for the percentage of males favoring the amendment and one for the percentage of females.

Background Information

The American Association for Public Opinion Research encourages the news media and pollsters to include at least the following eight elements when reporting the findings from surveys of public opinion:

(1) the identity of who sponsored the survey;
(2) the exact wording of questions;

Is it possible today for a black candidate to be elected governor of Michigan?

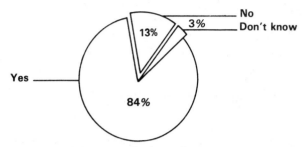

Are whites more or less likely to vote for Lucas because he's black?

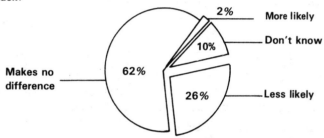

Are blacks more or less likely to vote for Lucas because he's black?

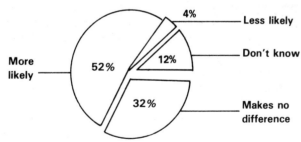

SOURCE: Adapted from charts that appeared in the **Detroit News,** September 14, 1986.

Figure 9.1: Example of Pie Charts: The Impact of Race on Campaign for Governor

    (3) a definition of the population sampled;
    (4) the size of the sample—for mail survey, this should include the number of questionnaires mailed out and the number returned;

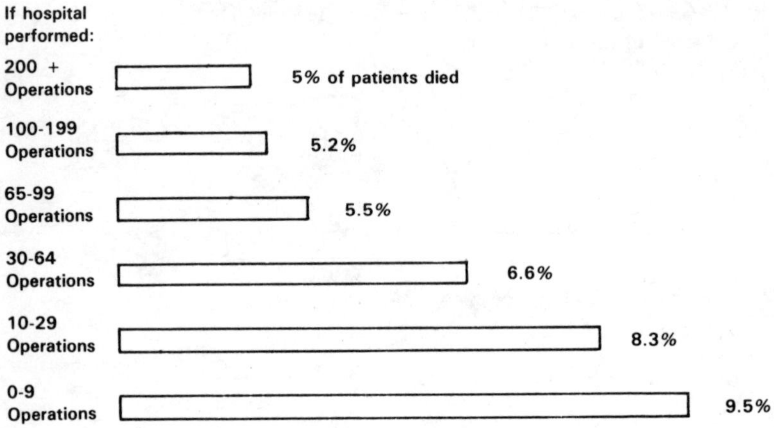

If hospital performed:

200 +
Operations ▭ 5% of patients died

100-199
Operations ▭ 5.2%

65-99
Operations ▭ 5.5%

30-64
Operations ▭ 6.6%

10-29
Operations ▭ 8.3%

0-9
Operations ▭ 9.5%

SOURCE: Adapted by permission from a graph appearing in the **Detroit Free Press,** September 21, 1986; data supplied by the American Association.

Figure 9.2: Example of a Bar Chart: Number of Medicare Coronary Bypass

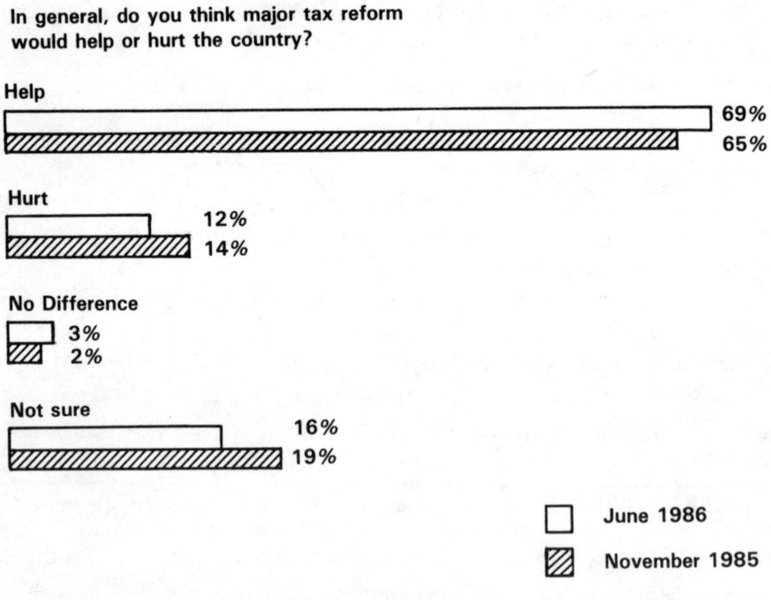

In general, do you think major tax reform
would help or hurt the country?

Help
▭ 69%
▨ 65%

Hurt
▭ 12%
▨ 14%

No Difference
▭ 3%
▨ 2%

Not sure
▭ 16%
▨ 19%

▭ June 1986
▨ November 1985

SOURCE: Adapted by permission of the **Wall Street Journal,** June 6, 1986.

Figure 9.3: Bar Chart Comparing Changes Over Time

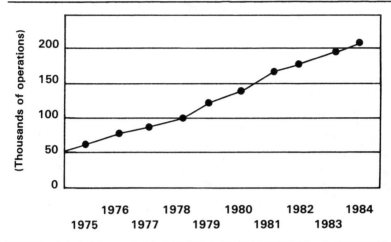

SOURCE: Adapted from a graph appearing in the **Detroit Free Press,** September 21, 1986; data supplied by the American Heart Association.

Figure 9.4: Example of a Line Chart: Heart Bypass Operations

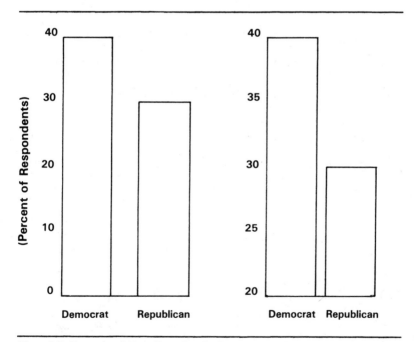

Figure 9.5: Example of How Data Can Be Distorted in a Bar Chart: Political Party Affiliation

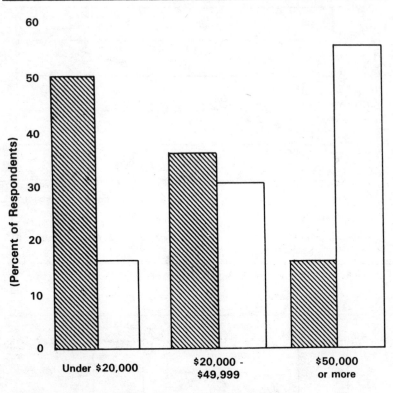

NOTE: Open box, Republicans; shaded box, Democrats.

Figure 9.6: Example of a Bivariate Bar Chart: Income of Republicans and Democrats

(5) those results based on parts of the sample, rather than on the total sample—for example, likely voters only, those aware of an event, those who answered other questions in a certain way;

(6) whether interviewing was done in person, by telephone, mail, or on street corners;

(7) when the interviewing was done in relation to relevant events; and

(8) an indication of what allowance should be made for sampling error.

In addition, we recommend including the response or return rate and, when applicable, a discussion of special problems that occurred during data collection. The background information can be incorporated into the main story or in a sidebar. The *Wall Street Journal*, for example, ran the following sidebar with its story reporting the results of a poll of the public's attitude toward tax reform.

The Wall Street Journal/NBC News poll is based on telephone interviews conducted June 2 and 3 with 1,599 adults.

The sample was drawn from 400 locations across the country. Individual households were selected by a probability-sample design that gave all telephone numbers, both listed and unlisted, a proportional chance of being included. One person, 18 years old or older, was chosen from each household by a systematic procedure to provide the appropriate balance between men and women.

Chances are 19 out of 20 that if all households with telephones in the U.S. had been surveyed using the same questionnaire, the results would differ from the poll findings by no more than three percentage points in either direction [June 6, 1986].[6]

ETHICS

No code of ethics has been adopted explicitly for precision journalists, but they, as all journalists, are guided by a strong sense of responsibility. Indeed, while conducting research for this book, we found no examples of outright distortion, fabrication, or capriciousness.

Still, a code of ethics represents a formal commitment to a set of principles and encourages journalists to be their own watchdogs. We would be remiss, therefore, not to include some discussion of a set of standards. For this, we again turn to the American Association for Public Opinion Research.

Members of the AAPOR pledge themselves to use care in developing their research designs and gathering and processing data, taking all reasonable steps to assure the accuracy of results. Findings and methods must be described accurately and in appropriate detail.

In addition AAPOR members pledge that when they become aware of distortions in their research, they will publicly disclose what is required to correct the distortions.

And, finally, the AAPOR code states that researchers must not lie or use practices and methods that abuse, coerce, or humiliate respondents. Unless respondents waive confidentiality, all comments are to be held as privileged and confidential, and their names will not be disclosed for nonresearch purposes. (See Appendix D.)

IDEAS FOR PROJECTS

In Chapter 1 we said that an idea for a precision-journalism project is generated in much the same manner as any other news story. Throughout this book, and especially in this chapter, we have discussed a number of projects. Now we would like to offer a more systematic overview of how ideas can be generated.

Ideas for Surveys

Public opinion polls usually deal with attitudes toward social problems and issues such as crime, health, discrimination, pornography, education, pollution, taxes, and welfare. These are certainly important. However, a poll may also be used for less serious or more entertaining issues. What do people do in their spare time? Where are their favorite places to vacation? What television shows do they watch most frequently?

Another twist is to poll occupational or social groups other than the general public. What do doctors think of the health-care system and the rising costs of health care? What do criminal lawyers think of the criminal justice system? Teachers of the educational system? Legislators of the political system? High school students toward drugs?

Since many news organizations regularly sponsor surveys, attitudes may also be tracked over time as public opinion can and does change. In the early 1970s, fewer than half of U.S. adults favored the death penalty for persons convicted of murder. Today, an overwhelming majority support such punishment. Following such trends provides interesting insights into changing social conditions and norms.

Ideas for Content Analysis

On the content-analysis front, the ideas are somewhat more constrained because a written record must be available.

You may have noticed that many of the examples of content analysis in this book have used criminal justice records. Crime, of course, is an important concern in nearly every major city. Its prominence as a research topic, however, also draws on the fact that there are so many public records available on the subject. Police, courts, and state administrative agencies have tons of records; most of them are open to public inspection. Although criminal justice issues are certainly important, governmental records are available on a multitude of other subjects—health care, taxation, the environment, licensing, education, international trade, and the like.

Some of the questions that can be asked are these: Do legislators vote according to their campaign promises? How often do they deviate from their political party's position on the issues? Where do they get their campaign finances? What are the leading causes of death in a community? Who is most likely to commit suicide and what are some correlates? How do tax assessments match up with sales data?

In Chapter 10 we take a look at how a team of reporters—some using precision journalism and others using traditional investigative reporting techniques—worked together to uncover the story of Michigan's "Revolving Door Prisons."

NOTES

1. The stories are part of an ongoing series about the criminal justice system in Chicago, which appeared in the *Chicago Tribune*, June 3 and 4, 1985. Copyrighted Chicago Tribune Company, all rights reserved, used with permission.

2. Reprinted with permission of the *Arizona Republic*. Permission does not imply endorsement by the newspaper.

3. Reprinted with permission of the Detroit Free Press.

4. Reprinted with permission of the Dallas Times Herald.

5. Reprinted courtesy of the *Charlotte Observer*.

6. Reprinted by permission of the *Wall Street Journal*, copyright Dow Jones & Company, Inc. (1986) All rights reserved.

A CASE STUDY

A Detroit Free Press precision-journalism project shakes up Michigan's correctional system.

By David Ashenfelter
Staff writer, Detroit Free Press

It was the crime that scuttled the Prison Overcrowding Emergency Powers Act and made Michigan angry enough to build prisons.

About 2:30 p.m. last Oct. 25, paroled murderer Wayne Lemarr Harvey and his girlfriend, an escapee from a Lansing halfway house, gunned down a policeman and then a housewife a few miles from the state Capitol.

The killings horrified the public and shocked state government. Within several weeks, Gov. Blanchard stopped using the Prison Overcrowding Emergency Powers Act to relieve prison overcrowding and the Legislature scrambled to build more prisons to handle the overflow. . . . [1]

It was also the crime that launched Ashenfelter, Michael Wagner, two other *Free Press* reporters, and a computer consultant into a nine-month precision-journalism project that examined how the Michigan Department of Corrections responded to the crisis of overcrowded prisons. The investigation resulted in a six-day, 16-page series called "Revolving Door Prisons."

Response to the series was swift and intense. Before it finished running, the House Corrections Committee ordered Michigan Department of Corrections officials to appear at a hearing and two parolees were rounded up and sent back to prison when correction officers discovered they had been released two years early. Within a week, the Democratic governor ordered an investigation of the situation and Senate Republicans began drafting a series of bills to correct abuses the series uncovered. Within a month, both houses of the legislature were conducting hearings and investigations in the Michigan criminal justice system and making recommendations for changes in policy and law.

Before the year was out, the Department of Corrections had repro-grammed its computer and changed its record-keeping procedures.

What did the reporters find that caused so much political upheaval and such swift change in the Michigan criminal justice system? The lead story on day one began:

Michigan criminals have been getting out of prison earlier than the law allows—some of them before serving even half their minimum sen-tences—as a result of the state's drastic measure to relieve prison overcrowding.

A *Free Press* investigation found that the Michigan Department of Corrections has broken at least two laws and circumvented several others in its 10-year struggle to flush inmates out of its badly clogged prison system.

Corrections officials have given thousands of inmates far bigger sentence reductions than they had coming under the law, weakened prisoner disciplinary policies and, at one point, imposed a quota on the number of unruly inmates that could be returned to prison from halfway houses.

The policies have helped Michigan become one of the few states in the country to control prison overcrowding in the past decade, but Michigan has paid a price. The state has created a turnstile system of justice that has exposed its residents to more crime and fostered cynicism and contempt among crime victims, judges, prosecutors, police officers—and the Corrections Department's own staff. . . .

Less than a month after the Harvey murders, Ashenfelter, under the provisions of the Michigan Freedom of Information act, petitioned the Department of Corrections for copies of its computer records. The seven tapes he eventually obtained contained the records of the 65,000 inmates who had been in the Michigan prison system since 1981—the year the department began using the computer to keep track of inmates.

At the same time, he began reading background material on how other states were handling prison overcrowding. He consulted with the Department of Corrections data analyst and a computer consultant at Wayne State University.

With the help of the consultant, Larry Kostecke, the tapes were fed into Wayne's computer so that the records of all the inmates paroled in 1983 could be isolated. Inmates paroled in 1983 were selected because research shows that parolees who get into trouble usually do so within 14 months of their release.

For five months Ashenfelter and Kostecke massaged, analyzed, and verified the massive data base they developed from the records of the

5,762 inmates parolled in 1983. They were able to determine how many got out of prison early, how many were returned to prison, and the types of new crimes they committed.

The records were incomplete and full of errors. The researchers had to verify and often correct the data by checking it against the paper files in the Department of Corrections record clerk's office. They developed a formula and a set of definitions and recalculated the sentences. They interviewed Department of Correction officials so they could sort out the meaning of the data and understand procedures. They ordered policy manuals from the department, again using the Michigan Freedom of Information Act.

Ashenfelter and Wagner studied the laws—good time, emergency powers act, disciplinary credits, mandatory gun term sentencing; they studied audit reports that criticized how the Department of Corrections handled good time and disciplinary credits. When they were done they found that, among other things:

- one-third of the inmates paroled in 1983 had been in trouble again by early 1985—12 of them had committed murder;
- 45% of the computerized sentence records for the parolees were incorrect;
- a combination of clerical and computer errors had resulted in dramatically reduced sentences for several inmates—one, for instance, got 40 months instead of 40 years;
- 80% of the prisoners were released before they had served their minimum sentence; and
- mandatory sentences for crimes committed with a gun were being illegally shortened.

While Ashenfelter and Kostecke were getting the computer data under control, special project reporters Wagner, Tom Hundley, and Laura Berman were out uncovering the story of halfway houses, the parole board, and a typical day in the prison system. Often they followed up on leads supplied by Ashenfelter and Kostecke as they spotted strange things in the computer data; often they alerted Ashenfelter and Kostecke to look for data verifying hunches they had from strange things happening in the field.

HOW THEY PRESENTED THEIR STORY

Although the credibility of the series rested on the findings from the computer analysis—and the stories and graphics that presented those findings (see Figure 10.1)—the impact was conveyed by the stories that

A STUDY OF 5,762 PAROLEES

These charts are based on Corrections Department records and a Free Press study of department records. The Free Press isolated information on 5,762 Michigan inmates who were paroled in 1983.

How well parole worked over the years

Year	Parolees	Failures	Percent
1973	3,614	1,212	33.5
1974	3,268	1,188	36.4
1975	3,044	1,190	39.1
1976	3,335	1,199	36.0
1977	4,122	1,489	36.1
1978	4,147	1,417	34.2
1979	4,303	1,405	32.7
1980	4,193	1,321	31.5
1983*	5,762	1,888	32.8

* Free Press study group as of Jan. 10, 1985. The other studies are follow-up studies conducted by the Michigan Department of Corrections Parole failures range from failure to report to parole officers to convictions for new crimes.

1983 parolees who got out early, by crime category

	Total number of parolees	How many left early	Percent
All crimes	5,762	4,711	81.8
Crimes against people	2,504	2,092	83.6
Crime against property	2,621	2,106	80.4
Drugs, weapons and others	637	513	80.5

794 new crimes by 1983's parolees

Of the 5,762 parolees of 1983, the Parole Board kept 18.2 percent in prison until they had served at least their minimum sentences. Were they really worse risks than the prisoners released early? Yes. The 1983 parolees had been convicted of 794 new crimes by Jan. 10, 1985, and the 18.2 percent held to full minimums or more committed 22.5 percent of them. Moreover, they were responsible for 29.6 percent of the new crimes against people.

Who did the new crimes?			
Crimes against people	55	131	186
Crimes against property	108	428	536
Drugs and other	16	56	72

Source: Free Press study

Figure 10.1: Examples of Tables Accompanying the *Free Press* Series

(continued)

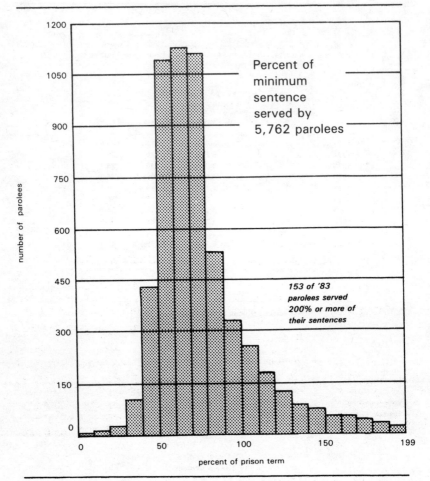

Figure 10.1 Continued

told the case histories of inmates who had been paroled early because of record-keeping errors. Some excerpts:

A paroled murderer and a female friend are in Washtenaw County Jail as suspects in the slayings of a couple in Dearborn and a man in Ypsilanti Township.

Alan Wilson Lumsden, 28, of Ypsilanti, who was paroled last October after serving 8 1/2 years of a 20-to-60 year prison term for second-degree murder, was charged Wednesday with carrying a concealed pistol in a

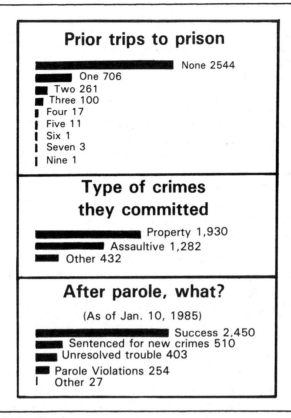

Prior trips to prison

None 2544
One 706
Two 261
Three 100
Four 17
Five 11
Six 1
Seven 3
Nine 1

**Type of crimes
they committed**

Property 1,930
Assaultive 1,282
Other 432

After parole, what?

(As of Jan. 10, 1985)

Success 2,450
Sentenced for new crimes 510
Unresolved trouble 403
Parole Violations 254
Other 27

Figure 10.1 Continued

motor vehicle and possession of a sawed-off shotgun. Lumsden—whose murder sentence was cut primarily because of "good time" he received despite poor conduct in prison—is held in lieu of $1 million bond . . . .

Less than six years after he had been given a 15-to-25 year sentence for rape, Theodore Meek was legally free, sitting in a bar in Utica, buying drinks for a woman he would kill a few hours later. . . .

Maxine Gray is a widow—a victim of Michigan's early release program. It happened suddenly in the comfort of the family room: Two men burst into her Bloomfield Township home at 8:18 on the evening of Feb. 9, 1984. Minutes later, one of them shot her 51-year-old husband at close range in the back of the head with a stolen .38 Charter Arms revolver. . . . "

The evening John Gray was shot, Michael Mrozek and Perry Bradley were driving from Detroit to Pontiac when they stopped to ply the only trade in which Mrozek said he'd known real success: Stealing from other people.

At the time, Mrozek was a 21-year-old armed robber, finishing his sentence at his brother's house in Pontiac. Because of a halfway house "population crunch," according to department records, he had been placed on extended furlough from custody six months before he was eligible for parole. . . .

All in all, Ashenfelter and Kostecke worked on the series for nine months, the other reporters, for five. The *Free Press* spent almost $8,000 for consulting services, the computer tapes, computer times, and manuals—not an exorbitant amount considering the $5,200 it cost the *Free Press* in 1967 for Philip Meyer to do the landmark precision-journalism project that analyzed the causes of the Detroit riots. But it would have cost much less if the state's inmates records had been in better order and if Ashenfelter had had previous experience working with computers. The cost to obtain the tapes: $417.91.

A REVIEW OF THE RESEARCH PROCESS

At the end of Chapter 1, we introduced the rest of the book by describing the steps in the research process. To close, we will dissect the *Free Press* investigation to see how it fits the model of a descriptive study.

The first stage, you will recall, was identified as interest and resources. The *Free Press* has a long history of allocating resources to in-depth investigative projects and in fact has a special-projects team of investigative reporters. These reporters had developed a long list of potential projects; the prison overcrowding issue was one of them. As noted earlier, it was the Harvey murders that propelled them into action.

The research idea—using computerized records held by the state—interestingly enough came from the work of a reporter for the rival newspaper, the *Detroit News*. Fred Girard had just completed a computer-assisted series using the records from the Department of Corrections. Ashenfelter called Girard to find out what records were there. That was when his ideas began to gel.

Defining concepts, the next step, was crucial to the study. One of the first things Ashenfelter and Wagner realized when they began examining the records was that they had to come up with a set of definitions so they could make sense of the data. Their concepts included such things as original sentence date, the amount of time in prison, whether a parole was a success or a failure, minimum sentence, and corrected sentence date.

The research method the reporters used was, of course, content analysis of public records, supported by traditional investigative-reporting techniques.

The reporters fielded the project by obtaining and analyzing computer tapes and cross checking them with the Department of Corrections's paper files.

Because the research was based on the entire population of 1983 parolees, rather than on a sample, the reporters' data analysis relied on descriptive statistics—percentages, frequencies, and means. Although their data analysis was limited to description, they were able to provide interpretation from the background information they gathered and from their sources.

It should be noted that the project would have taken much less time and would have cost much less if indeed a sample of the parolees had been used. The reporters would have had much less data to analyze and verify and they would have saved money by using a personal computer rather than renting Wayne State University's mainframe computer. If they had done so, they undoubtedly would have come up with much the same results—if, as we pointed out in our discussion of sampling theory in Chapter 4, every inmate paroled in 1983 had been given an equal chance of being selected for the sample.

But, also as we pointed out in Chapter 4, studying an entire population is always better because there is no chance of sampling error. It is also true that by studying the entire population, the reporters were able to flesh out the individual cases that contributed to the impact of the series.

Nevertheless, any news organization, even ones with much tighter budgets than that of the *Free Press*, could successfully field a project such as this as long as the researchers were careful to use appropriate research methods and statistics.

The presentation of the results, as detailed earlier, was a week-long series of stories, graphs, charts, and photos that won an impressive list of awards, including the Society of Professional Journalist/Sigma Delta Chi Distinguished Service Award for Public Service.

NOTES

1. This and all other excerpts from the series reprinted with permission of the *Detroit Free Press*.

APPENDIX A

Random Numbers

When you need a Table of Random Numbers, such as when you are drawing a sample through the random digit dialing method, you can almost always find one in a statistics or research textbook (see next page), or you can generate your own using a personal computer and a simple *Basic* program. For example, if you needed 100 numbers printed out you would enter:

```
10 RANDOMIZE
20 For I=1 to 100
30 LPRINT FIX (10000*RND);
40 NEXT I
RUN
```

When you type "RUN," the program asks you, "random number seed (-32768 to 32767)?" Enter any number in the indicated range. The program will generate 100 random numbers. A different "seed" number will give you a different set of numbers.

If you should want 1,000 random numbers, you would revise lines 20 and 40:

```
20 For I-1 to 1000
40 LPRINT FIX (1000000)*RND);
```

Note that the number in parenthesis in Line 40 is always 1,000 times as large as the number of random numbers you are asking for in Line 20. If you want the numbers printed on the terminal screen rather than on paper, substitute "PRINT" for "LPRINT" in Line 30.

The following random numbers were generated using the program just described. Let's see how it could be used to generate a random-digit-dialing sample. Assume the sampling frame consists of all of the telephone numbers in a city and that one area code covers the entire city. The first step is to make a list of all of the prefixes, the first three digits of the telephone numbers, in the area. Next, put the prefixes into a hat and randomly select one. To give the prefix a suffix, randomly start anywhere on the random numbers table and select four digits from a row and a column. Put the prefix into the hat and select again. Go to the table and select another suffix. The four numbers can be selected in any pattern because they themselves were randomly generated. Continue doing this until you have the required number of telephone numbers.

Table of Random Numbers

7473351	5980634	4952806	6429234	1196117
6181966	2739921	0394547	9820196	1249670
7216986	0422826	1856942	1274687	1236172
8582552	9225909	6123351	8323482	4920721
9911108	7468635	6584993	5744097	3117249
3321403	5113114	4400458	6925997	5061661
2892829	4559848	8452222	6969804	0207952
5995827	6500244	8257867	2547374	2866719
6720087	7600778	7011317	4496865	9263730
0167605	1217576	8657873	8941352	7152804
4707778	7349863	7877588	7807475	2853628
5082724	0667774	3970608	3263157	9657359
2034201	7100331	4686976	5446937	6982362
7805165	8424524	9178143	3457202	7875272
2230316	8212426	7499372	4813703	6720198
1327252	0901474	8867651	4277592	1997354
1364314	2559699	0459750	4175978	5153150
2719070	7904001	0576136	2253944	5012878
2734001	3451858	4029612	0977379	3465987
7879436	3376271	7549218	2415021	7538681
0648195	3824266	4317415	4648881	2596745
8801371	9417840	1752393	6571853	3519114
7835410	1287279	6104402	3009845	7598081
9794676	9695980	7393803	1470135	9606738
8475127	8910366	5858432	2127884	6353585
1449307	2218660	3616047	2682552	2582036
0961586	3463929	7408926	8092855	7859305
4980245	8731560	9010207	2951489	8670976
3257510	1137923	1951640	8020620	8658285
7086479	0153337	7773440	8826096	0804237
8836487	4714713	1530108	4608704	4173575
0951984	8572690	8717774	8635915	9696312
8445663	3280984	4899898	3543522	1486551
2910761	2253245	5255456	7534832	3713671
5501252	1041219	6088187	2821673	6373046
6338434	8958749	0423366	7427831	4094489
5429356	4295238	8461140	5547786	9909796
6832920	5411082	3508995	2093064	4582433
1764596	8142300	9611606	0271436	2463699
5246651	3193571	7340483	0311735	7037015
4319062	6974264	4879628	5425623	5376384
7632865	3912128	7803221	2318296	7083007
7234064	5320323	9818260	6929306	3156594
3668456	8926692	9645516	7383452	6361415

(continued)

APPENDIX A Continued

7227208	8105782	4417203	0516510	1492881
7615892	1465488	5135815	2842485	0444521
4847277	1887422	4396748	2854487	8899117
8386686	1434600	4633998	7381385	3977480
4049425	1127902	7384535	8013442	2305309
7768940	5735348	0639224	3893294	7108990
7903186	6071746	4287621	8350324	9406236
8381443	9401988	9376851	9717766	9773514
0745794	1285375	8672369	1369176	3080391
5416838	5372220	6486909	4575335	2887572
9593318	6423712	9464635	6620551	5691744
8736346	3203003	5876640	9009903	8022590
0122103	3285843	4782782	9202488	3586804
4378556	9544194	3299599	8651428	9616815
5033031	5722249	7215998	8925547	4599512
7044778	5682492	8723818	2111436	6288793
5111091	1456088	3360427	6704416	3876428
7623454	9968191	4051535	2823841	0314907
5792759	7381053	2925620	2238575	5834742
2316139	5437257	5252980	7643579	6833477
4553699	2398282	5223785	9544518	2565596
2527534	5441206	0476728	7515549	6837927
6929265	4354837	3354365	9402045	1495212
6382094	2597303	8199111	8026376	0521510
1480324	0146240	8896416	0277114	7616343
8029686	8871566	1975200	0151479	0036095
6516889	0545578	2421302	1783754	8102527
7802823	7107088	0853838	4009951	3227525
3892064	3821665	7638207	7247541	9617660
5787944	6810172	7019243	0939760	2410022
7678800	4708769	9484951	4433140	1133373
8273273	9506773	4721676	1705752	4742172
8041970	7790402	8976625	5998402	7566738
1835729	1481758	7059662	1152975	3266958
3118246	6859670	0124535	3737532	2050763
1529405	4213473	9676284	2117809	0178366
4216299	4318687	6737962	3175814	7150223
2238106	5316132	2932029	3909411	6377045
2149802	7179554	9421231	7578400	7835286
4754448	5302505	6616708	3173977	3877537
5015757	8729395	5578593	2935662	1525464
0648028	7979432	3762930	7454307	0129565
0230621	7421961	7739419	7987605	3016363
2485144	4788639	2623638	4257191	5815883
6136755	7058293	8016215	5849846	4601762

(continued)

APPENDIX A Continued

8462590	5905374	8376217	0941104	0189191
0991684	4818947	9007933	6303648	4203490
3018003	3407349	8615652	3236714	0510614
9652659	6210288	3961108	0312529	6821622
7479278	4326502	9199259	2712700	4652237
0769051	8487334	1501307	0827919	7117491
7315548	3896062	9505471	5999387	8426209
9795036	6615678	2747379	6446393	3442003
5052217	1805437	8669191	1082692	1702906
5635110	8334959	1121032	6980952	6121772
0412569	6775407	6856204	8480879	9880660
1234905	7386402	7664211	2508884	5315566
1748425	7266131	8139160	7616631	9769544
0929826	6466923	7176799	9958669	6253563
5322373	8630468	4037603	1196936	1451726
9863991	3972288	2987118	3798463	2171924
1504058	9525111	9284582	2913274	0180885
3291994	1091845	0667755	9888634	7755173
9443030	2892031	3882309	6274634	4883182
6075971	8317307	3509191	4060860	8398895
4280664	9322735	8009389	4885828	2322306
5190485	2928109	5063748	9486300	3105241
3463628	3117835	8842105	6983627	8491068
0547723	1515819	6572347	9395316	1323750
1221432	3854435	0852275	9543204	1292073
1955500	4110115	9586579	4211263	6549981
2770519	8773822	3644163	9767395	1069939
2520582	8968824	6598585	4660840	1994462
2307440	3801976	3892953	4271266	8057593
1309818	9594526	4991254	4923507	6134439
1353572	3515388	0447296	8774498	8299117
0581583	8040215	2121230	2382457	8460958
6513909	2864698	4158402	3614082	2111665
5400043	1066525	1847231	3039659	8233736
8212419	5968632	6498209	2889825	1648939
5944716	8213023	5316184	4157457	1556367
4466449	9790769	3529112	7555172	6628727
5327862	3346057	1319670	8189236	4584323
6262710	3011605	4287747	5265840	9787006
8232173	3745672	4033180	4561646	3178274
3597311	2908438	5145345	2298760	6121107
7379493	9096681	9601246	2994168	2470552
1950945	9156130	2476487	2082676	1437327
8228722	5163496	6807296	1406535	8391898
6961565	7050294	6265918	9548612	8786833
8188259	5510715	6338146	7346454	8224730

(continued)

APPENDIX A Continued

0755307	7042361	8419845	7946450	5264462
4991945	2639942	3579616	5984594	2472664
3774445	1946127	8075003	7131613	9507070
8119835	1939131	0883466	4718797	5582797
2755813	1316722	7269125	8881521	2510520
5599962	6277316	8783218	4526619	6888092
2903648	9932055	0496613	3228598	3630664
1005399	0013398	8967794	6044426	7370071
2601510	8657070	7115758	6238596	2248377
3459147	3981500	4325451	4435564	0054322
7225759	8003318	5670031	2046722	6661158
5959329	5515376	3870550	9610083	4351322
1123089	7196339	1685939	4464087	4263798
9837199	0074394	2865617	0858525	7155069
9314633	4063358	3009931	5966964	9580605
5660459	3533567	0951231	7462278	6012024
2989127	3553792	9246881	4381358	9211692
3394397	6700163	3596220	9342986	2172876
5347636	5205070	4362625	0075386	5255828
7133326	6119362	4680663	4313533	3839604
6862344	2366269	4013062	8971977	1272355
2214847	7731488	0524218	0993074	2420367
1511903	8492054	1662318	9194375	7344663
5029418	2443293	8172248	8948641	7104692
8055850	8319441	0052474	1656963	3307728
8337734	5175815	3252272	0125805	5571490
2910583	4239861	7087354	7413896	1702213
7408428	1451284	5213218	8130906	1142370
3689398	0679053	07692876	7078042	4517638
4788571	8081606	00259997	4427337	9192775
4969092	1797246	5716468	0122743	0287097
4019501	7020897	4795883	3008399	8133425
0345627	0322180	2428043	4378888	0596055
5110448	3944588	4685211	7609216	2774578
7341359	7827417	0685037	8539789	7567697
7082486	56117586	8148881	8020208	0385596
4226321	9268478	6324015	2986383	6387340
5395284	2614005	2605183	4564632	2262333
0316081	7089285	0841328	6745234	9428413
4569184	6450948	8268426	2302685	6114826
3808652	2711426	1925347	0891859	1042494
8815077	2698865	3817887	9024664	7087804
3722971	5718715	0902747	1211856	4575911
5984601	4130966	1949564	3595698	7726509
5001434	3549584	8661361	5432353	5675408
2653151	0474193	5123250	3714532	9700330
8339005	7009773	4112092	2836261	8445370

APPENDIX B
Sampling Error Estimates for 95% Level of Confidence

Sample Size	5% 95%	10% 90%	15% 85%	20% 80%	25% 75%	30% 70%	35% 65%	40% 60%	45% 55%	50% 50%
					Observed Value					
50	6.0	8.3	9.9	11.1	12.0	12.7	13.2	13.6	13.8	13.9
75	4.9	6.8	8.1	9.1	9.8	10.4	10.8	11.1	11.3	11.3
100	4.3	5.9	7.0	7.8	8.5	9.0	9.3	9.6	9.8	9.8
150	3.5	4.8	5.7	6.4	6.9	7.3	7.6	7.8	8.0	8.0
200	3.0	4.2	4.9	5.5	6.0	6.4	6.6	6.8	6.9	6.9
250	2.7	3.7	4.4	5.0	5.4	5.7	5.9	6.1	6.2	6.2
300	2.5	3.4	4.0	4.5	4.9	5.2	5.4	5.5	5.6	5.7
350	2.3	3.1	3.7	4.2	4.5	4.8	5.0	5.1	5.2	5.2
400	2.1	2.9	3.5	3.9	4.2	4.5	4.7	4.8	4.9	4.9
450	2.0	2.8	3.3	3.7	4.0	4.2	4.4	4.5	4.6	4.6
500	1.9	2.6	3.1	3.5	3.8	4.0	4.2	4.3	4.4	4.4
550	1.8	2.5	3.0	3.3	3.6	3.8	4.0	4.1	4.2	4.2
600	1.7	2.4	2.9	3.2	3.5	3.7	3.8	3.9	4.0	4.0
650	1.7	2.3	2.7	3.1	3.3	3.5	3.7	3.8	3.8	3.8
700	1.6	2.2	2.6	3.0	3.2	3.4	3.5	3.6	3.7	3.7
750	1.6	2.1	2.6	2.9	3.1	3.3	3.4	3.5	3.6	3.6
800	1.5	2.1	2.5	2.8	3.0	3.2	3.3	3.4	3.4	3.5
850	1.5	2.0	2.4	2.7	2.9	3.1	3.2	3.3	3.3	3.4
900	1.4	2.0	2.3	2.6	2.8	3.0	3.1	3.2	3.3	3.3
950	1.4	1.9	2.3	2.5	2.8	2.9	3.0	3.1	3.2	3.2
1,000	1.4	1.9	2.2	2.5	2.7	2.8	3.0	3.0	3.1	3.1
1,100	1.3	1.8	2.1	2.4	2.6	2.7	2.8	2.9	2.9	3.0
1,200	1.2	1.7	2.0	2.3	2.5	2.6	2.7	2.8	2.8	2.8
1,300	1.2	1.6	1.9	2.2	2.4	2.5	2.6	2.7	2.7	2.7
1,400	1.1	1.6	1.9	2.1	2.3	2.4	2.5	2.6	2.6	2.6
1,500	1.1	1.5	1.8	2.0	2.2	2.3	2.4	2.5	2.5	2.5
1,750	1.0	1.4	1.7	1.9	2.0	2.1	2.2	2.3	2.3	2.3
2,000	1.0	1.3	1.5	1.8	1.9	2.0	2.1	2.1	2.2	2.2
2,500	.9	1.2	1.4	1.6	1.7	1.8	1.9	1.9	2.0	2.0
3,000	.8	1.1	1.3	1.4	1.5	1.6	1.7	1.8	1.8	1.8

NOTE: See Chapter 8 for more information.

APPENDIX C
Critical Values of Chi-Square

Degrees of Freedom	Level of Confidence		
	90%	95%	99%
1	2.71	3.84	6.63
2	4.61	5.99	9.21
3	6.25	7.81	11.35
4	7.80	9.49	13.28
5	9.24	11.07	15.05
6	10.64	12.59	16.81
7	12.02	14.07	18.48
8	13.36	15.51	20.09
9	14.68	16.92	21.67
10	15.99	18.31	23.21
11	17.28	19.68	24.73
12	18.55	21.03	26.22
13	19.81	22.36	27.69
14	21.06	23.68	29.14
15	22.31	25.00	30.58
16	23.54	26.30	32.00
17	24.77	27.59	33.41
18	25.99	28.87	34.81
19	27.20	30.14	36.19
20	28.41	31.41	37.57
21	29.62	32.67	38.93
22	30.81	33.92	40.29
23	32.01	35.17	41.64
24	33.20	36.42	42.98
25	34.38	37.65	44.31
26	35.56	38.89	45.64
27	36.74	40.11	46.96
28	37.92	41.34	48.28
29	39.09	42.56	49.59
30	40.26	43.77	50.89

NOTE: See Chapter 8 for more information.

APPENDIX D

Code of Ethics of the American Association for Public Opinion Research

[Revised January 15, 1986]

We, the members of the American Association for Public Opinion Research, subscribe to the principles expressed in the following code. Our goal is to support sound practices in the profession of public opinion research.

We pledge ourselves to maintain high standards of scientific competence and integrity in our work, and in our relations both with our clients and with the general public. We further pledge ourselves to reject all tasks or assignments which would be inconsistent with the principles of this code.

THE CODE

I. Principles of Professional Practice in the Conduct of Our Work

   A. We shall exercise due care in gathering and processing data, taking all reasonable steps to assure the accuracy of results.

   B. We shall exercise due care in the development of research designs and in the analysis of data.

      1. We shall recommend and employ only research tools and methods of analysis which, in our professional judgment, are well suited to the research problems at hand.

      2. We shall not select research tools and methods of analysis because of their capacity to yield a misleading conclusion.

      3. We shall not knowingly make interpretations of research results, nor shall we tacitly permit interpretations, which are inconsistent with the data available.

      4. We shall not knowingly imply that interpretations should be accorded greater confidence than the data actually warrant.

   C. We shall describe our findings and methods accurately and in appropriate detail in all research reports.

II. Principles of Professional Responsibility in Our Dealings with People

   A. The Public

      1. We shall cooperate with legally authorized representatives of the public by describing the methods used in our studies.

      2. When we become aware of the appearance in public of serious distortions of our research, we shall publicly disclose what is required to correct the distortions.

B. Clients or Sponsors

   1. When undertaking work for a private client, we shall hold confidential all proprietary information obtained about the client's business affairs and about the findings of research conducted for the client, except when the dissemination of the information is expressly authorized by the client or becomes necessary under terms of Section II-A-2.

   2. We shall be mindful of the limitations of our techniques and facilities and shall accept only those research assignments which can be accomplished within these limitations.

C. The Profession

   1. We shall not cite our membership in the Association as evidence of professional competence, since the Association does not so certify any persons or organizations.

   2. We recognize our responsibility to contribute to the science of public opinion research and to disseminate as freely as possible the ideas and findings which emerge from our research.

D. The Respondent

   1. We shall not lie to survey respondents or use practices and methods which abuse, coerce, or humiliate them.

   2. Unless the respondent waives confidentiality for specific uses we shall hold privileged and confidential all information that tends to identify a respondent with his or her responses. We shall also not disclose the names of respondents for non-research purposes.

[Reprinted by permission of the American Association for Public Opinion Research.]

FURTHER READING

BABBIE, EARL R. (1986) *The Practice of Social Research* (4th ed.). Belmont, CA: Wadsworth.

Babbie's book is one of the most popular introductory research textbooks in the social sciences. It contains an excellent introductory discussion of how scientists go about testing causal models.

BAILEY, KENNETH D. (1978) *Methods of Social Research.* New York: Free Press.

Besides the required discussion of methodology and statistics, Bailey's text includes a relatively easy-to- understand discussion of how to construct theories. (See Chapter 19).

BOHRNSTEDT, GEORGE W. and DAVID KNOKE (1982) *Statistics for Social Data Analysis.* Itasca, IL: F.E. Peacock.

This book is more technical and demanding than most introductory statistics textbooks, but, as such, is an indispensible reference manual. It contains the formulas for the most widely used statistics.

FELGENHAUER, NEIL (1972) "Precision journalism, " pp. 65-75 in Everette E. Dennis (ed.) *The Magic Writing Machine: Student Probes of the New Journalism.* Edited by Everette E. Dennis. Eugene, OR: University of Oregon Press.

Feigenhauer's article examines the philosophy and history of precision journalism.

FOWLER, FLOYD J., JR. (1984) *Survey Research Methods.* Newbury Park, CA: Sage.

This text deals exclusively with survey research methods. The author covers the problems encountered in data collection and the solutions researchers use to overcome them.

HAGE, GEORGE S., EVERETTE E. DENNIS, ARNOLD H. ISMACH, and STEPHEN HARTGEN (1983) *New Strategies for Public Affairs Reporting.* Englewood Cliffs, NJ: Prentice-Hall. This reporting textbook includes one of the best introductory discussions of precision journalism available. (See Chapter 5.)

HANDEL, JUDITH D. (1978) *Introductory Statistics for Sociology.* Englewood Cliffs, NJ: Prentice-Hall.

Handel's text offers a thorough introductory discussion of elementary descriptive and inferential statistics. It also briefly covers multivariate statistics.

McCOMBS, MAXWELL, DONALD LEWIS SHAW, and DAVID GREY (eds.) (1976) *Handbook of Reporting Methods.* Boston: Houghton Mifflin.

This book contains a number of articles written by mass communication researchers for journalists interested in social-science research methods. Some of the topics it covers are surveys and polls, sampling, interviewing, participant observation, field experiments, and the nature of news.

MEYER, PHILIP (1979) *Precision Journalism: A Reporter's Introduction to Social Research Methods* (2nd ed.). Bloomington: Indiana University Press.

Meyer's book, published originally in 1973, was the first comprehensive work on precision journalism. It is an excellent reference manual.

REYNOLDS, H. T. (1977) *Analysis of Nominal Data.* Newbury Park, CA: Sage.

This is one of more than 50 books available through Sage's "Quantitative Applications in the Social Sciences" series. Each book deals with a separate research topic or statistical technique.

RYAN, MICHAEL and JAMES W. TANKARD JR. (1977) *Basic News Reporting.* Palo Alto, CA: Mayfield.

Chapter 11 in this introductory reporting text provides a good introduction to precision journalism.

WEISS, CAROL H. (1972) *Evaluation Research.* Englewood Cliffs, NJ: Prentice-Hall.

This book is a crucial reference manual for journalists who need to understand how governmental programs are evaluated through social-science research methods.

WILLIAMS, FREDERICK (1979) *Reasoning with Statistics.* New York: Holt, Rinehart and Winston.

This book, according to the author, is intended for people who need to be knowledgeable readers of quantitative research literature in their fields, but who lack the necessary statistical background. The discussion of multivariate statistics avoids weighty mathematical formulas.

WIMMER, ROGER D. and DOMINICK, JOSEPH R. (1987) *Mass Media Research: An Introduction* (2nd ed.). Belmont, CA: Wadsworth.

This book discusses research methods and the use of statistics in a media-oriented context.

INDEX

ABOUT THE AUTHORS

DAVID KEVIN PEARCE DEMERS is teaching reporting courses and working toward his Ph.D. in journalism and mass communication at the University of Minnesota. After completing his undergraduate education at Central Michigan University, he spent four years reporting for several newspapers in Michigan. During that time he earned two statewide awards for investigative reporting. He became interested in precision journalism while studying in the Kiplinger Program in Public Affairs Reporting at the Ohio State University. After graduation he continued his studies in research and methodology at Ohio State, earning a master's degree in sociology. Before entering Minnesota he was a research analyst for a national marketing research company. He has been involved in more than 100 survey research projects and is currently conducting research on newspaper editors' attitudes toward opinion polling. He and Mona Rae Pearce were married earlier this year.

SUZANNE NICHOLS has been on the faculty of the Journalism Department at Central Michigan University since 1969, teaching writing, reporting, and editing. She has also taught journalism research and advertising at the University of South Dakota. Throughout the years, she has been involved in a variety of social survey and content analysis research projects. Before she began her college teaching career, she earned a master's degree in journalism from the University of Wisconsin—Madison and worked as a reporter for the University of Wisconsin Extension Division News Bureau and the Vermillion (South Dakota) *Plaintalk*.

NOTES

NOTES

NOTES